SO-ARO-702

Holiday Decorations

Toys & Favors

WITH PRICES

PUBLISHED BY

L-W BOOK SALES

P.O. Box 69
Gas City, Indiana 46933

Second Printing 1994

INDEX

HALLOWE'EN NOVELTIES
PUMPKIN LANTERNS

27131   27007

		GROSS
641/138	Miniature Pumpkin Lantern, well made, 2 inches	$4.50
641/100	Pumpkin Lantern, 3½ inches	3.90
27131	Pumpkin Lantern, 4¼ inches	4.50
27003	Pumpkin Lantern, 4¾ inches	7.80
27132	Pumpkin Lantern, 5 inches	9.25
27133	Pumpkin Lantern, 5½ inches	11.40

		DOZEN
27005	Pumpkin Lantern, 7½ inches	$1.85
27006	Pumpkin Lantern, 9 inches	2.90
641/105	Pumpkin Lantern, 10½ inches	4.20
641/106	Pumpkin Lantern, 12 inches	12.60

COMIC NOVELTY LANTERNS

H1   641/107

		DOZEN
27007	Comic Pumpkin Lantern with Jap Lantern Hat, 4 inches	$.72
27008	Comic Pumpkin Lantern with Jap Lantern Hat, 5 inches	1.35
725/316	Comic Pumpkin Lantern with Jap Lantern Hat, 6 inches	2.10
725/317	Comic Pumpkin Lantern with Jap Lantern Hat, 7 inches	3.00
27137	Comic Pumpkin Lantern with folding Jap Lantern, 4 inches	1.95
27135	Comic Pumpkin Lantern with Large Nose and Ears, 3½ inches	.70
27009	Comic Pumpkin Lantern with Large Nose and Ears, 4½ inches	1.25
27136	Comic Pumpkin Lantern with Large Nose and Ears	1.90
27152	Comic Face, Flat Pumpkin Lantern, 4¼ inches	.85
27151	Comic Face Witch Kettle Lantern with 3 Legs and Handle, 7½ inches	2.10
10893	Comic Red Devil Face Lantern, 3½ inches	.95
H1	Black Cat Head Lantern, 3½ inches	.42
H3	Black Cat Head Lantern, 5 inches	.80
641/107	Skull Head Lantern, 3 inches	.38
641/108	Red Devil Head Lantern, 3 inches	.38
641/111	Red Devil Head Lantern, 4 inches	.80
18762	Large Witch Head Lantern. Well made, 18 inches	24.00
18763	Large Devil Head Lantern. Well made, 15 inches	24.00
18764	Large Skull Head Lantern. Well made, 14 inches	24.00

HALLOWE'EN NOVELTIES (Continued)
FOLDING PAPER LANTERNS

		GROSS
11686	Round Folding Paper Lantern, asst. Hallowe'en Designs, 4¾ inches....	$3.60
11687	Oval Shape Folding Paper Lantern, asst. Hallowe'en Designs, 7 inches	6.60
11688	Ball Shape Folding Paper Lantern, asst. Hallowe'en Designs, 6 inches	4.35
11689	Ball Shape Folding Paper Lantern, asst. Hallowe'en Designs, 8 inches	7.80
11690	Ball Shape Folding Paper Lantern, asst. Hallowe'en Designs, 10 inches	12.60
11685	Round Flat Comic Face Folding Paper Lantern. Very Attractive for Store and Dance Hall Decoration, 25 inches......................	DOZEN $3.25

		GROSS
11682	Hallowe'en Folding Fan with Black Cat Design, 10 inches......................	$3.00
32/159	Hallowe'en Paper Fan with Cricket and Wooden Handle, 11 inches......	6.60

COMIC FIGURES

| 11687 | | 25108 | | 11685 |

		GROSS
25018	Fur Body Pumpkin Figures, Arms and Legs on Springs, 3 inches........	$4.50
30/110	Same as 25018 but 4½ inches.....	7.20
25143	Comic Black Cat with Wire Legs and Tail on Springs, 2½ inches........	4.80
4005	Celluloid Figures, asst. Vegetable Heads, attractively colored, 3½ inches	5.40
25051	Hallowe'en Roly Poly Figures, assorted, 1½ inches......................	4.20
25151	Comic Pumpkin Figure with Vegetable Body, 2 inches......................	4.20
7032/101	Comic Assorted Hallowe'en Figures on Springs, 2½ inches..................	7.20
27149	Comic Hallowe'en Boy Figures, assorted on box, 2¾ inches.................	4.80
25152	Witch Sitting on Black Cat, mounted on box, 3 inches......................	4.80
27121	Red Devil Figure with Pumpkin Body on box, 4 inches......................	7.20
5704	Red Devil Paper Figures, 4 inches......................	5.40
5713	Paper Comic Pumpkin Figures, 5 inches......................	8.40
5718	Paper Comic Clown Dressed Pumpkin Figures, 5 inches......................	9.60
27148	Comic Figures on Box, assorted, 3 inches......................	5.40
25157	Witch and Black Cat Dancing Figures on Box, 3 inches......................	8.40
641/185	Assorted Devil, Ghost, Black Cat and Pumpkin Comic Figures with Cloth Dress, box, 5 inches......................	8.40
4000	Comic Hallowe'en Boxes, 6 attractive assorted styles each about 3 inches, wonderful value	4.00
4001	Suit Case with Pumpkin Face, 2½ inches. Box......................	4.00
4002	Hallowe'en Candlestick with Pumpkin Face, Box, 3 inches......................	4.00
4003	Comic Hallowe'en Figures, Candlesticks, Pumpkins, Black Cats, etc., mounted on box, each about 5 inches, good value......................	8.40
72236	Same as 4003 above but about 5½ inches......................	9.25
40/715	Black Witch Hat with Braid. Box, 4 inches......................	5.40
4004	Comic Hallowe'en Figures with Squeaker, 3½ inches......................	4.80
4006	Round Box, with Silk Covered Top, Pumpkin and Black Cat Heads, 2 inches	10.20

Holiday Decorations 1995 Price Guide

ALL ITEMS IN THE FOLLOWING PRICE GUIDE ARE PRICED IN VERY GOOD CONDITION. EACH PRICE IS FOR 1 OF AN ITEM. ALL PRICES ARE THE OPINION OF THE EDITOR AND WE TAKE NO RESPONSIBILITY FOR GAINS OR LOSSES IN USING THIS GUIDE.

Page 3

Pumpkin Lanterns 3 1/2-5 1/2"	$50+
Pumpkin Lanterns 7 1/2-12"	$40+
Comic Pumpkin Lanterns	$40+
Comic Witch-Red Devil	$60+
Black Cat Lanterns	$80+
Scull-Devil Lanterns	$50+
Lrg. Witch-Devil-Skulls	$100+

Page 4

Folding Paper Lanterns	$20+
Folding Fans	$15+
Comic Figures	$30+
Boxes-Small 1-3"	$30+
Boxes-Large 3"+	$40+
Other Items	$25+

Page 5

Comic Figures	$25+
Boxes-Small 1-3"	$30+
Boxes-Large 3"+	$45+
Red Devil Boxes	$75+
Comic Novelties 2-3"	$25+
Comic Novelties 3"+	$30+

Page 6

Comic Novelties 3"+	$40+
Painted Comic Squeakers	$40+

Page 7

Pumpkin Boxes-Small	$40+
Pumpkin Boxes-Large	$50+
Balloons	$10+
Pins	$15+

Page 8

Pins	$15+
Black Cats	$40+

Page 9

All Black Cats	$45+
Decorated Boxes	$30+

Page 10

Novelties	$25+
Instrument Boxes-Small	$45+
Instrument Boxes-Large	$50+

Page 11

Halloween Noisemakers	$15+

Page 12

Halloween Noisemakers	$15+

Page 13

Surprise Favors	$5+
Halloween Novelties	$10+

Page 14

Miniature Novelties	$5+
Fortune Telling Sets	$50+
Fortune Telling Games	$50+

Page 15

Masks	$15+
Hats	$25+

Page 16

Kewpie Dolls	$50+
Larger Celluloid Kewpie	$125+

Page 17

China Kewpies	$100+
Halloween Kewpies/Box	$125+
Decorations Etc.	$15+

Page 18

Halloween Cutouts	$15+
Seals, Napkins, Etc.	$2+

Page 19

Halloween Mottoes	$10+
Elsco Mottoes	$10+
Large Mottoes	$15+

Page 20	
Jack Horner Pies	$50+
Halloween Nut Cups	$20+

Page 21	
Turkeys	$30+
Cheaper Quality	$10+

Page 22	
Roast Turkeys	$10+
Fruit Baskets	$10+
Other Novelties	$10+

Page 23	
Thanksgiving Novelties	$10+
Miniature Plates	$25+
Thanksgiving Mottoes	$15+
Elsco Snapping Mottoes	$15+

Page 24	
Thanksgiving Novelties	$2+
Seals, Table Covers, Etc.	$2+
Jack Horner Pies	$30+
Nut Cups & Ice Creams	$5+

Page 25	
Dressed Kewpie Dolls	$30+
Footballs Imit. Leather	$15+
Football Favors	$5+
Kewpie Football Players	$50+

Page 26	
Santa Claus	$50+
Santa on Boxes	$60+
Painted Trouser Figures	$60+
Cloth Trouser Figures	$75+
Stooping Position Figures	$75+
Santa & Music Box	$100+

Page 27	
Santa Claus Figures	$80+
Santa Claus on Boxes	$100+
Red Cotton Figures	$100+
Celluloid Figures	$50+

Page 28	
Santa Figures	$35+
Novelty Boxes	$25+
Snow Baby	$80+

Snowball	$30+
Wooden Santa Figure	$100+

Page 29	
Christmas House	$50+
Comic Novelties	$50+
Santa Claus Masks	$20+
Santa Suite	$100+

Page 30	
Snow Children	$75+
Snow Children on Sleds	$100+
China Snow Figures	$100+

Page 31	
Papier-Mache Reindeer	$60+
Metal Reindeer	$40+
Celluloid Reindeer	$20+
Paper Reindeer	$15+
Reindeer Drawing Sled	$100+

Page 32	
Containers Only	$25+
Filled Stockings 10½-15½"	$100+
Filled Stockings 18-26"	$150+
Filled Bags	$100+
Baskets, Sleds, Boxes	$10+

Page 33	
Folding Trees 16-28"	$60+
Folding Trees 32-54"	$80+
Favor Christmas Trees	$20+
Seals, Tags	$1+
Cabinet-Complete	$200+

Page 34	
Dressed Kewpies 2½"	$50+
Dressed Kewpies 3½"	$60+
China Kewpies	$75+

Page 35	
Kewpies on Glazed Boxes	$100+
Large Dressed Kewpies	$100+
Santa Dressed Kewpie	$150+
Holly Sprays & Poinsettias	$5+
Red Parasols	$5+

Page 36	
Snapping Mottoes	$20+

Elsco Snapping Mottoes	$15+	Metal Kazoos	$4+
		Metal Horns	$5+
Page 37		Musical Bells	$4+
Elsco Snapping Mottos	$15+		
Jumbo Mottoes	$25+	Page 46	
Jack Horner Pies	$200+	Balloon Noisemakers	$2+
		Blowouts	$2+
Page 38		Wooden Noisemakers	$5+
Silver Tinsel Garlands	$5+ box		
Ribbon Icicles	$4+	Page 47	
Angel Hair & Lametta	$5+	Wooden Noisemakers	$5+
Christmas Snow	$5+	Comic Noisemakers	$5+
Candleholders & Fasteners	$5+		
Glass Icicles & Balls Ea.	$5+	Page 48	
Icicles (Full Card)	$20+	Confetti Etc.	$5+
		Fireworks	$25+
Page 39			
Tinsel Garland	$10+	Page 49	
Tinsel Ornament	$10+	Paper Hats	$5+
Tinfoil Ornament	$5+		
Houses, Ornaments	$15+	Page 50	
Cornucopias & Boxes	$25+	Paper Hats	$5+
Folding Boxes	$10+		
		Page 51	
Page 40		Favors	$15+
Paper Bells	$3+		
Garlands	$3+	Page 52	
Fibre Rope Garlands	$10+	Favors to Fill	$25+
Santa Claus Bag	$$40+		
		Page 53	
Page 41		Favors to Fill	$25+
Cases for Nuts	$5+	Novelty Fancy Boxes	$35+
Cases for Ice Cream	$7+		
		Page 54	
Page 42		Outdoor Sport Favors	$50+
New Year Favors	$10+	Fruit & Nut Containers	$25+
Miniature Bottles	$15+		
		Page 55	
Page 43		All on Page	$50+
Glass Containers	$50+		
Souvenir Novelties	$5+	Page 56	
		Favors (Heart Boxes)	$15+
Page 44		Decorated Heart Boxes	$20+
Noisemakers	$5+	Red Satin Boxes	$15+
Whistles	$2+	Red Boxes, Well Made	$15+
Harmonicas	$5+		
		Page 57	
Page 45		Misc. Novelty Boxes	$40+
Horns	$2+	Comp. Footballs	$10+
Cow Bells	$5+		

HALLOWE'EN NOVELTIES (Continued)
COMIC FIGURES

		GROSS
31/300H	Open Celluloid Parasol Hallowe'en Color, 2½ inches	$8.40
31/301H	Open Celluloid Parasol Hallowe'en Color, 3½ inches	10.20
641/172	Comic Pumpkin Face Figure Holding Pumpkin on Wire, 4½ inches..	14.40
355/96	Comic Black Cat with Ribbon Bow on Round Box, 2¾ inches	7.20
520/176	Pumpkin Head with Stem on Box, 2 inches	4.50
520/174	Comic Hallowe'en Crepe Paper Figures, 6 assorted styles with squeaker and removable head, 5½ inches	8.40
641/200	Witch Figure with Pumpkin Head, Holding Cat, Box, 4 inches	10.20

		DOZEN
27042	Comic Witch and Black Cat Figures, Box, 6 inches	$1.45
27113	Comic Figures Dressed as Vegetables on Round Box, 4½ inches	1.20
27041	Comic Witch and Black Cat Figures, Box, 4½ inches	.75
25133	Pumpkin and Black Cat Roly Poly Figures, 2¼ inches	1.25
25159	Comic Witch Figure, well made, 4½ inches	1.60
725/119	Comic Witch with Black Cat, Removable Head, 3¾ inches	.80
520/221	Paper Comic Witch Figure Box, 5¼ inches	.75
725/355	Assorted Comic Hallowe'en Figures Nicely Colored, Box, 4¼ inches	1.00
H1295	Assorted Comic Hallowe'en Figures Nicely Colored, Box, 8 inches....	1.75

RED DEVIL BOXES

		DOZEN
10830	Red Devil Head Box, well made, 2 inches	.60
10891	Red Devil Head Box, well made, 3¼ inches	1.20
10901	Comic Red Devil with Shaking Horns on Box, 4¼ inches	.85
10892	Comic Red Devil Figure with Shaking Horns and Removable Head, 5½ inches	1.50

COMIC NOVELTIES
Beautifully Hand Colored and Well Made

725/304   25135   520/215

		GROSS
10850	Hallowe'en Comic Painted Face Hat Box, assorted colors, 2¾ inches	$8.40
10819	Hallowe'en Comic Painted Face Hat Box, 2¼ inches	9.60
725/353	Hallowe'en Open Basket with Handle, 3 inches	7.80
520/215	Comic Face Paper Pumpkin with Witch Hat Box, 5 inches	9.90
520/218	Comic Face Paper with Candlestick Hat Box, 5½ inches	9.00

		DOZEN
725/296	Painted Comic Pumpkin Head in Basket, 3 inches	$1.00
725/297	Painted Comic Pumpkin Head in Basket, 4½ inches	1.70
25182	Painted Comic Pumpkin Head on Round Box, 3½ inches	1.50
25145	Painted Comic Pumpkin Head on Round Box, 3 inches	1.50
10851	Comic Face Pumpkin Color Basket with Handle, 4 inches	.75
725/304	Comic Face Mushroom Shape Box, 4 inches	1.30
25132	Kerchief Basket with Pumpkin Face Box, 3 inches	1.50
25138	Painted Comic Pumpkin Face Squeaker, 3½ inches	1.85
25124	Painted Comic Pumpkin Face House with Chimney on Box, 4 inches	2.00
725/300	Comic Face Pumpkin with Long Wire Legs on Box, 6½ inches	1.90
25135	Comic Face Cucumber Figure with Long Wire Legs on Box, 6 inches	2.10
725/302	Comic Face Carrot Figure with Long Wire Legs on Box, 8¼ inches	2.05

HALLOWE'EN COMIC NOVELTIES (Continued)

		DOZEN
10848	Comic Face Pumpkin with High Hat, Box, 3 inches	$1.00
H1128	Comic Face Pumpkin with High Hat, Box, 4 inches	1.50
10852	Comic Face Black Cat, Box, 3 inches	1.20
725/306	Comic Face Pumpkin Figure Box, well made, 6¼ inches	1.25
725/307	Comic Face Black Cat Figure Box, well made, 6¼ inches	1.25
25142	Comic Witch Figure with Paper Dress and Hat, 7½ inches	2.20
25140	Comic Pumpkin Head on Tub Shaped Box with Two Handles, 5 inches	1.80
725/298	Brown Pumpkin Box with Comic Ghost Face, 3¾ inches	1.75
641/160	Comic Wooden Pumpkin Jumping Jack with Vegetable Shaped Arms and Legs, 6½ inches	3.60

HAND PAINTED COMIC FACE SQUEAKERS

725/105

25165

725/104

		GROSS
725/104	Painted Comic Pumpkin Face Squeaker, 2½ inches	$11.40
725/110	Painted Comic Devil Face Squeaker, 2½ inches	11.40
725/107	Painted Comic Witch Face Squeaker, 2½ inches	12.60
725/109	Painted Comic Black Cat Face Squeaker, 2½ inches	11.40
		DOZEN
725/106	Painted Comic Pumpkin Face Squeaker, 3½ inches	$1.50
725/108	Painted Comic Black Cat Face Squeaker, 3½ inches	1.60
725/105	Painted Comic Pumpkin Face Squeaker with Long Legs on Stand, 4½ inches	1.60
725/111	Painted Comic Pumpkin Face Squeaker with Long Legs on Stand, 5½ inches	2.25
725/117	Painted Comic Pumpkin Face House Squeaker on Round Box, 5½ in.	2.50
725/112	Painted Comic Double Pumpkin Face Squeaker with Ribbon for Hanging, 4½ inches	1.95
725/116	Painted Comic Pumpkin Face Squeaker with Ribbon for Hanging, 6¼ inches	3.30
725/115	Painted Comic Pumpkin Face Squeaker with Feet, 6¼ inches	3.50
725/113	Painted Comic Pumpkin Face Squeaking Box, 3½ inches	1.63
725/114	Painted Comic Pumpkin Face Squeaking Box, 4½ inches	2.50
725/299/1	Painted Comic Pumpkin Face Chime Box with High Hat, 5¼ inches	1.95
725/299/2	Painted Comic Pumpkin Face Chime Box with High Hat, 7¾ inches	2.95
25127	Comic Pumpkin Head on Squeaking Pumpkin, 5 inches	1.85
25128	Witch Head on Round Squeaking Pumpkin, 5 inches	2.10
25129	Comic Black Cat Head on Round Squeaking Pumpkin, 5 inches	2.10
90	Comic Face Pumpkin on Round Box with Black Hat Squeaker, 5 inches	1.65
725/303	Painted Comic Face Mushroom Shape Squeaker, 2¾ inches	1.35
725/216	Comic Face Black Cat Inside Comic Face Pumpkin Squeaker, 3¾ in.	1.00
725/217	Comic Face Black Cat Inside Comic Face Pumpkin Squeaker, 4¾ in.	1.75
		DOZEN
25165	Painted Comic Pumpkin Face Sprinkler Can Horn, 6½ inches	$2.75
520/217	Hallowe'en Table Box Decorated with Two Comic Face Pumpkins, 4½ inches	1.00
25193	Hand Painted Comic Face Carrot Figure Dancing on Round Box, 6½ inches	4.20
25192	Hand Painted Comic Face Pumpkin Figure Dancing on Round Box, 6½ inches	4.20
25191	Hand Painted Comic Face Black Cat with Pumpkin Figure on Round Box, 6½ inches	4.20

HALLOWE'EN NOVELTIES (Continued)
COMIC PUMPKIN HEAD BOXES

		GROSS
	25027 H1258	
520/213	Crepe Paper Pumpkin Box with Painted Comic Face, 2¾ inches.........	$4.35
25027	Comic Face Pumpkin Head Box, 2 inches......................	5.40
27153	Painted Comic Face Pumpkin Head Box with Stem, 2¾ inches.............	8.40
641/169	Comic Face Pumpkin Head with Green Leaf, 2½ inches....................	9.60
		DOZEN
641/140	Comic Face Pumpkin Head with Green Stem, Box, 3½ inches...............	$1.50
H1257	Comic Face Pumpkin Head with Green Stem, Box, 4½ inches...............	2.40
H1258	Comic Face Pumpkin Head with Green Stem, Box, 6¼ inches..............	4.80
641/143	Comic Face Pumpkin Head with Green Stem, Box, 7¼ inches...............	10.80
25160	Comic Face Pumpkin Stein Shape Box, well made, 5¼ inches...............	6.90
27160	Wax Pumpkin Box, well made in natural color, 1½ inches...............	.35
27050	Wax Pumpkin Box, well made, 2½ inches....................	.75
27051	Wax Pumpkin Box, well made, 3 inches......................	1.00

COMIC HALLOWE'EN BALLOONS AND PINS

		GROSS
32/442	Yellow Pumpkin Shape Rubber Balloon, with Painted Face and Patent Valve, 4 inches......................	$4.50
32/444	Yellow Rubber Balloon with Painted Black Witch Cats and Wooden Squawker, 6 inches	5.40
32/186	Black Cat Rubber Balloon with Large Face and Legs. When blown up has arched back and squeaks, 7 inches.....................	9.60
32/270	Yellow Rubber Balloon with Painted Pumpkin, when squeezed makes sound like barking dog, 6 inches......................	10.20
		DOZEN
32/397	Comic Figure with Comic Face Rubber Balloon. Squeaks when squeezed, 12 inches	$2.20

10816	27069	520/101	27078

		GROSS
641/174	Hallowe'en Assorted Comic Head Pins, 1½ inches...................................	$1.80
520/182	Black Witch Cat with Shaking Tail on Pin, 1½ inches..........................	2.40
807	Paper Comic Pumpkin Head Pin with Orange and Black Sunflower, 2½ inches	3.00
5715	Paper Comic Pumpkin Head Pin with Black and Orange Star, 2¾ inches	3.00
520/177	Wooden Pumpkin Figure Pin, Wire Arms and Legs, 2 inches	3.60
520/178	Wooden Black Cat Figure Pin, Wire Arms and Legs, 2 inches.............	3.60
520/179	Wooden Skelton Figure Pin, Wire Arms and Legs, 2 inches.................	3.60
520/180	Painted Wooden Witch Figure Pin, Wire Arms and Legs, 2 inches......	3.60
520/181	Painted Wooden Devil Figure Pin, Wire Arms and Legs, 2 inches......	3.60

HALLOWE'EN NOVELTIES (Continued)
HALLOWE'EN PINS

		GROSS
520/101	Painted Skeleton Figure Pin with Wire Arms and Legs, 2 inches	$3.60
806	Pumpkin Head Pin with Large Feather, 4 inches	3.75
5716	Pumpkin Head Pin on Orange and Black Daisy	3.90
10816	Hallowe'en Pin with Assorted Vegetable Heads, 1½ inches	4.20
27129	Jointed Wood Pumpkin Figure Pin, 2½ inches	4.50
27073	Wooden Pumpkin Figure Jumping Jack Pin, 2½ inches	4.50
27072	Wooden Skeleton Figure Jumping Jack Pin, 2 inches	4.50
27128	Wooden Jointed Black Cat Figure Pin, 2¼ inches	4.50
27069	Wooden Black Cat Figure Jumping Jack Pin, 1¾ inches	4.80
27081	Painted Witch Figure Holding Black Cat, 2 inches	4.80
27077	Assorted Vegetables on Pins with Wire Arms and Legs, 2 inches	4.80
27078	Comic Pumpkin Head on Green Leaf with Three Small Pumpkins on Wire Arm, 2½ inches	5.04
641/214	Comic Pumpkin Face on Pin with Moveable Tongue, 2½ inches	7.80
641/190	Comic Pumpkin Face on Pin with Long Wire Horns, 4 inches	7.80
10894	Comic Pumpkin Face Pin, Jointed Arms and Legs. 2¾ inches	8.40
313	Paper Snapper on Pin Decorated with Witch Figure, 3 inches	5.04
295	Paper Pumpkin Head Pin Snapper, 4 inches	7.80

BLACK CATS

641/155	641/177	431/121	GROSS

		GROSS
25143	Comic Black Cat with Wire Legs on Springs, 2½ inches	$4.80
10863	Comic Black Cat with Shaking Head on Round Base, 2¼ inches	4.32
25117	Comic Black Cat on Round Box, 2½ inches	4.80
1007	Black Witch Cat Charm, 1 inch	4.80
27124	Black Cat with Wire Tail on Pumpkin, 1½ inches	4.80
641/170	Black Cat Standing on Comic Face Pumpkin, 2½ inches	7.20
4752	Comic Black Cat, made with a Thistle, 3 inches	7.20
25156	Comic Black Cat with Long Tail, 2¼ inches	7.80
431/121	Comic Black Cat with Shaking Head on Round Base, 3 inches	7.80
725/326	Comic Black Cat on Pin with Long Shaking Tail, 3 inches	7.80
641/159	Comic Black Cat with Necktie and Shaking Head on Round Box, 3¼ inches	7.80
310a	Pressed Paper Black Cat with Wire Whiskers, Snapper, 3 inches	7.80
811	Chenille Black Cat with Long Bushy Tail, 3½ inches	7.80
812	Chenille Black Cat with Long Bushy Tail, 5½ inches	13.20
25154	Flannel Covered Black Cat, well made, 3 inches	9.60
2433/11	Metal Black Cat, splendidly made, 1½ inches	9.60
520/219	Black Cat with Wire Shaking Tail. "The Lucky Black Cat," each in Box, 3 inches	8.70
520/220	Same as 520/219 above but size, 5¼ inches each in box	15.00
H1298	Comic Black Cat Sitting on Comic Face Pumpkin, Box, 4 inches	9.00
431/122	Comic Black Cat with Shaking Head on Round Box, 3¾ inches	10.20
641/154	Comic Black Cat with Long Rubber Neck, 2½ inches	10.20
641/177	Comic Black Cat on Chimney, Box, 3 inches	10.80

		DOZEN
H1240	Comic Black Cat with Long Rubber Neck, Box, 5 inches	1.25
25155	Flannel Covered Black Cat with Long Tail. Box well made, 5½ inches	1.75
H1241	Comic Black Cat with Long Rubber Neck, Box, 10¼ inches	6.90

HALLOWE'EN NOVELTIES (Continued)
BLACK CATS

9040 10856 9087

Fur Cloth Cats with Arched Backs and Long Tails Splendidly Made. Very Natural Looking.

		DOZEN
10853	Fur Cloth Black Cat, Glass Eyes and Whiskers, 9 inches	$6.35
10854	Fur Cloth Black Cat, Glass Eyes and Whiskers, 10 inches	8.70
10855	Fur Cloth Black Cat, Glass Eyes and Whiskers, 11 inches	12.00
10856	Fur Cloth Black Cat, Glass Eyes and Whiskers, 13 inches	19.80
431/104	Fur Cloth Black Cat, Glass Eyes, Cheaper Quality, 4 inches	2.00
725/276	Fur Cloth Black Cat, Glass Eyes, Cheaper Quality, 5½ inches	3.60

All of the Above Have Removable Heads for Filling.

		DOZEN
5788/5	Black Velvet Cat with Glass Eyes and Long Tail, Orange Ribbon Rosette Around Neck, Splendid Quality and Very Attractive, 6½ inches	3.60
5788/6	Yellow and Black Velvet Cat, same as above but size, 7½ inches	6.90
37/338	Black Velvet Squeaking Cat, Long Bushy Tail and Bow around Neck, 8 inches	6.00
37/339	Black Velvet Squeaking Cat, Long Bushy Tail and Bow around Neck, 10 inches	7.80

NOVELTY HALLOWE'EN DECORATED BOXES

		DOZEN
9034	Miniature Dress Suit Case, with Hallowe'en Labels, 1½ inches	$.35
9035	Miniature Dress Suit Case, with Hallowe'en Labels, 2 inches	.40
9036	Miniature Dress Suit Case, with Hallowe'en Labels, 2½ inches	.45
9037	Miniature Dress Suit Case, with Hallowe'en Labels, 3 inches	.75
9039	Miniature Satchel with Pumpkin Face, 2 inches	.85
9040	Miniature Satchel with Pumpkin Face, 3 inches	1.05
9030H	Hallowe'en Cigarette Case with Black Cat Pictures, 3¼ inches	.40
9032	Hallowe'en Cigarette Case with Black Cat and Pumpkin Pictures, 3¾ inches	.75
9123	Hallowe'en Telescope Cover Boxes, Assorted Shapes and Pictures, 2½ inches	.70
9079	Round Blocked Pumpkin Color Box with Comic Face Picture, 2¼ in.	.75
9075	Pumpkin Color Boxes, Assorted Shapes and Pictures, 3 inches	.80
9068	Pumpkin Color Boxes, Assorted Shapes and Pictures, 2½ inches	.70
9081	Pumpkin Color Boxes, Assorted Shapes and Pictures, 3½ inches	1.05
9038	Pumpkin Color Steamer Trunk with Black Cat Pictures, 3¼ inches	1.45
520/216	Pumpkin Color Book Box with Black Cat Decoration, 4½x3½ inches	.85
33/116	Pumpkin Color Slide Box with Assorted Hallowe'en Pictures, 3½x2¾ in.	.70
33/118	Pumpkin Color Steamer Trunk with Hinged Cover and Clasp, Decorated with Black Straps and Black Cat Pictures, 4x2½ inches.	1.00
355/100	Square Pumpkin Color Box with Assorted Hallowe'en Pictures, 1¾ in.	.50
3051	Lantern Shape Box with Comic Pumpkin Face and Handle, 3 inches.	.40
9174	Pumpkin Color Round Boxes with Assorted Pictures, 2¼ inches	.70
9175	Pumpkin Color Round Boxes with Assorted Pictures, 4 inches	1.50
9176	Pumpkin Color Round Boxes with Assorted Pictures, 5½ inches	2.00
9159	Hallowe'en Candlestick with Comic Pumpkin Face, 2½ inches	1.25
9160	Hallowe'en Candlestick with Comic Pumpkin Face, 3½ inches	1.65
9150	Hallowe'en Hat Box with Comic Face Picture, Straps and Handle, 2¼ inches	1.00

9

HALLOWE'EN NOVELTIES (Continued)

Well Made Novelty Hallowe'en Decorated Boxes for Filling. Attractively
Finished with a Lace Paper Liner. Very Distinctive.

9161

9153

		DOZEN
9087	Hallowe'en Book Box Decorated with Comic Pumpkin Face, 3 inches.	$1.70
9136	Pumpkin Color Book Box with Black Trimmings and Assorted Black Cat Pictures, 8½ inches	2.25
9153	Lantern Shape Pumpkin Color Box with Black Trimmings and Handle and Comic Pumpkin Face Pictures, 3 inches	1.45
9155	Same as above 9153 but size, 4¾ inches	3.20
9161	Hallowe'en Candlestick with Comic Pumpkin Face, 5½ inches	2.70
9041	Gent's Miniature Hat Box with Straps and Comic Pumpkin Face, 1¾ inches	1.00
9135/3	Gent's Miniature Hat Box with Straps and Comic Pumpkin Face, 3 inches	1.70
9135/4	Gent's Miniature Hat Box with Straps and Comic Pumpkin Face, 4 inches	2.40
355/99	Pumpkin Color Round Box with Three Small Pumpkins on Cover, 2¾ inches	1.15
93/239	Pumpkin Color Clock Box with Comic Face, 4 inches	1.70
93/230	Crepe Paper Covered Round Box with Black Witch Cat, 4 inches	4.20
355/94	Miniature Flour Bag with Comic Hallowe'en Figure, 4 inches	.85
25174	Oval Shape Wooden Box with Comic Pumpkin Face, 4½ inches	2.25
25170	Comic Dancing Black Cat Figure on Round Box, Nicely Colored, 10½ inches	10.80
25169	Comic Dancing Pumpkin Figure on Round Box, Nicely Colored, 10½ inches	10.80

Well Made Miniature Musical Instrument Boxes Attractively Decorated with a Lace Paper Liner.

9139/2

9139/1

		DOZEN
9140/1	Decorated Banjo, 4 inches	$1.00
9140/2	Decorated Violin, 4 inches	1.00
9140/3	Decorated Mandolin, 4 inches	1.00
9139/1	Decorated Banjo, 5½ inches	1.50
9139/2	Decorated Mandolin, 5½ inches	1.50
9139/3	Decorated Banjo, 6 inches	1.50
9142	Decorated Round Rattle with Handle, 8 inches	2.25
9138/3	Decorated Banjo, 9 inches	3.25
9138/1	Decorated Violin, 9 inches	2.90
9138/2	Decorated Mandolin, 9 inches	2.90

10

HALLOWE'EN NOISEMAKERS

11652   1166/1

		GROSS
1166/1	Round Hallowe'en Double Rattle, with Cat and Pumpkin, 5 inches......	$4.00
1166/2	Square Hallowe'en Double Rattle, with Cat and Pumpkin, 5½ inches.	4.00
107	Hallowe'en Pipe Horn, Decorated with Pumpkins, 6½ inches...............	5.04
113	Cardboard Horn, Decorated with Pumpkins, 9½ inches............................	2.40
112	Cardboard Horn, Decorated with Pumpkins, 18 inches............................	4.00
11652	Cardboard Horn with asst. Hallowe'en Pictures and Fringed Ends, 16 inches	3.90
11651	Cardboard Horn with asst. Hallowe'en Pictures and Fringed Ends, 28 inches	7.20
109	Cardboard Horn with Pumpkin Pictures, Comic Pumpkin Head and Fringed Ends, 16 inches...	9.00
35/304	Hallowe'en Horn, Heavy Cardboard, 7½ inches..	4.32
35/305	Hallowe'en Horn, Heavy Cardboard, 14½ inches..	9.25
1166/6	Hallowe'en Blowout, Assorted Comic Pictures, 15 inches......................	1.80
11669	Hallowe'en Blowout, Assorted Comic Pictures with Feather and Whistle, 21 inches	3.00
1166/10	Hallowe'en Blowout, Assorted Comic Pictures with Feather and Whistle, 40 inches..	6.60
120	Pumpkin Face with Blowout, 20 inches..	4.50
27052	Round Comic Face Pumpkin Head Blowout with Feather and Whistle, 21 inches	9.25
520/222	Wooden Broom Whistle with Black Cat, 10 inches.................................	5.04
127	Comic Pumpkin Face Squeaker with Moving Eyes, 2½ inches.............	4.50
128	Comic Pumpkin Face Squeaker with Moving Tongue, 2½ inches........	4.50
10864	Comic Witch Head Squeaker with Moving Tongue, 2½ inches.............	4.80
520/175	Comic Hallowe'en Squeaker, 6 assorted styles, 4½ inches......................	4.50
97	Hallowe'en High Hat Squeaker with Elastic String, 2¾ inches...........	7.20
119	Comic Pumpkin Face Rattle and Horn, 6½ inches...................................	4.80
124	Comic Pumpkin Face Mama Horn, 4½ inches...	4.80
725/331	Comic Pumpkin Figure Squeaker, with Moving Tongue, 4 inches........	7.80
641/161	Comic Pumpkin and Vegetable Figure Squeaker with Moving Tongue, 6 inches	9.00
520/174	Assorted Comic Hallowe'en Figure Squeakers, 5 inches	8.40
725/177	Comic Face Hallowe'en Rattles, Assorted, 9 inches................................	7.80

111   35/300

		GROSS
570/4	Comic Face Double Pumpkin Squeaker, 3 inches...............................	$3.60
570/5	Comic Face Double Pumpkin Squeaker, 4 inches...............................	8.40
570/6	Comic Face Double Pumpkin Squeaker, 5½ inches.............................	13.20
		DOZEN
111	Vegetable Shape Horn, Assorted Styles, 9 inches............................	$1.70
25119	Comic Pumpkin Face Pipe Horn, 4½ inches.....................................	1.90
18759	Comic Pumpkin Face Pipe Horn, 6½ inches.....................................	2.25
25166	Comic Black Cat Face Pipe Horn, 6½ inches...................................	2.25
25163	Pumpkin Color Pipe Horn, 4 inches..	1.00
25120	Pumpkin Color Pipe Horn, 6½ inches...	1.65

11

HALLOWE'EN NOISEMAKERS
(Continued)

C3238

25071   115

		GROSS
C3238	Comic Pumpkin Face Pipe Horn, Wonderful Value, 5½ inches	$12.00
520/232	Comic Black Cat Squeaker, 4½ inches	10.20
35/300	Pocket Cat Cry When Squeezed, Crys Like Cat, 2¼ inches	9.25
25114	Comic Pumpkin Face Tambourine, 5 inches	10.20
121	Comic Pumpkin Face Ratchet Rattle, 5 inches	8.40
25071	Wooden Ratchet with Assorted Comic Figures, 10 inches	9.60
115	Wooden Ratchet with Comic Face Pumpkin Head, 8 inches	9.60
122	Comic Face Pumpkin Head, Ratchet Rattle, 6½ inches	12.00
355/44	Pumpkin Color Carrot Horn with Fringe End, 7 inches	13.20
35/306	Combination Paper Hat and Horn, 10 inches	9.60
641/215	Comic Face Pumpkin Head Rattle, 6 inches	8.40
98/15	Wooden Round Double Clapper with Black Cat Picture, 6½ inches	6.00
98/14	Wooden Oval Double Clapper with Witch Picture, 6½ inches	6.00
32/447	Pumpkin Color Wooden Clapper with Hallowe'en Pictures, 6 inches	8.70
725/104	Hand Painted Comic Pumpkin Face Squeaker, 2½ inches	11.40
725/109	Hand Painted Comic Black Cat Face Squeaker, 2½ inches	11.40

		DOZEN
725/106	Hand Painted Comic Pumpkin Face Squeaker, 3½ inches	$1.50
725/108	Hand Painted Comic Black Cat Face Squeaker, 4 inches	1.50
725/112	Hand Painted Double Comic Pumpkin Face Squeaker, 4½ inches	1.95
25164	Miniature Pumpkin Color Sprinkler Can Horn, 3½ inches	1.75
725/256	Comic Pumpkin Face Musical Chime Box with Handle, 6½ inches	1.10
725/257	Comic Pumpkin Face Musical Chime Box with Handle, 8½ inches	1.75
641/157	Musical Hallowe'en Accordeon Comic Witch and Black Cat Standing on Top—when played figures dance, 10 inches	3.75

725/112   641/157

		DOZEN
641/217	Comic Face Pumpkin Squeaking Figure with Feather Blowout, 6½ inches	$3.30
725/237	Comic Face Pumpkin Squeaking Figure, when pressed plays cymbals, 10½ inches	3.60
725/236	Comic Face Pumpkin Head Whistling Figure with Black High Hat and Long Wooden Handle, 14 inches	3.00
725/216	Comic Face Pumpkin with Black Cat Squeaker, 3½ inches	1.00
725/217	Comic Face Pumpkin with Black Cat Squeaker, 4½ inches	1.75

HALLOWE'EN SURPRISE FAVORS

		DOZEN
	295 520/100 310A	
310A	Black Cat, with favor and snapper, 2½ inches...	$.65
295	Pumpkin Head, with favor and snapper, on pin, 3 inches.......................	.65
37	Stork and Cupid Rider, with favor and snapper, 4½ inches...................	.65
14305	Champagne Bottle, with snapper and favor, 3½ inches...........................	.60
14302	Red Heart, with snapper and favor, 2¼ inches.......................................	.40
14310	Walnut, with snapper and favor, 1½ inches...	.35
14306	Imitation Chocolate, contains favor, 1 inch..	.30
14304	Gilt Paper Pistol, contains favor and snapper, 4½ inches.....................	.60
601/662	Cigar, with favor, 4 inches..	.60
11869	Cork, with 5 dice, 1½ inches...	.60
601/661	Chocolate Eclair, contains favors, 4½ inches...	1.20
32/3	Surprise Walnuts, real walnut shell, contains little novelties and motto verses	GROSS $4.00
		DOZEN
700	Magic Orange, containing cotton favors and balls, 2 inches...................	$1.35
701	Magic Apple, containing cotton favors and balls, 2 inches...................	1.35
702	Magic Pumpkin, containing cotton favors and balls, 2 inches................	1.35
706	Magic Candles, containing cotton favors and balls, 4 inches................	1.35
705	Magic Flower Pots, containing favors, 2½ inches...................................	.70
14301	Magic Camera, containing cotton favors and balls, 2 inches.................	.85

HALLOWE'EN NOVELTIES

		GROSS
520/100	Witch Broom Pencil, 6½ inches...	$4.50
27108	Wood Scissor Toy, with comic pumpkin head, 12 inches.......................	4.80
520/102	Spider, with wriggling legs on string, 2½ inches...................................	4.80
520/103	Chenille Spiders, assorted colors, 2 inches..	4.50
641/206	Black Cats, sitting on fence, movable, 8 inches.....................................	9.00
641/218	Comic Pumpkin Face Scissor Toy, 14 inches...	9.60
641/208	Comic Face Pumpkin Jack (Box), very amusing toy, 2½ inches..........	12.00
641/203	Dominoe Box, with comic face pumpkin Jumping Jack, 4½ inches....	12.00
16747	Pressed Paper Owl, 3½ inches..	12.00
		DOZEN
60/1013/1	Long Wooden Snake, flexible body, 17 inches.......................................	$ .75
60/1013	Long Wooden Snake, flexible body, 24 inches.......................................	1.00
2936	Long Wooden Snake, jointed body, 24 inches...	.85
520/104	Paper Snake, 24 inches...	1.00
725/336	Painted Wooden Jointed Snake, on pin, 4½ inches...............................	.60
601/65	Rubber Snake, natural color, well made, 7½ inches..............................	1.10
601/64	Rubber Snake, natural color, well made, 14 inches..............................	2.10
60/1012/1	Mechanical Wood Snake, 12 inches...	1.80
1200	China Skull Head Ash Receiver, 2¼ inches..	1.45
1202	China Skull Head Ash Receiver, 3¼ inches..	3.00
3043	China Cute Boy Figure with comic face pumpkin on stand, ash receiver, attractively colored, 3¾ inches...	1.35
3041	China Cute Boy Figure with comic face pumpkin and black cat on stand, well made and attractively colored, 5¼ inches..............................	2.70
13728	Comic Face Pumpkin Eyeglasses with open eyes, 4¼ inches.................	.25
3920	Comic Face Pumpkin Figure, cotton net bag, 8 inches.........................	1.00

13

MINIATURE HALLOWE'EN NOVELTIES

		GROSS
16700	Miniature Money Bag ($5000), 1¼ inches	$5.04
32/100	Black Mice on Pin, 2 inches	2.40
8063	Metal Beetle Cricket, 2 inches	.90
4107	Green Paper Frog, 2½ inches	3.00
16744	Green Frog on Ladder, 2 inches	2.00
12500	Heart Shape Thermometer, 1½ inches	4.80
32/273	Walking Bug on Wheels, 3 inches	4.50
		DOZEN
12732	China Devil, with Book and Vase, 1¾ inches	$1.25
32/236	Crawling Mechanical Bugs, 6 Different Styles, Assorted, 2 inches	1.80
32/237	Crawling Mechanical Moths, Assorted Colors, 2 inches	1.80
32/294	Crawling Mechanical Turtle, Assorted Styles, 2½ inches	1.80
32/295	Crawling Mechanical Fur Covered Beaver, 5 inches	4.00
32/297	Parrots on Swing Made of Peanut, Assorted Colors, 6 inches	2.70
16023	Skull Head Charm Pencil, 1¾ inches	1.80
16015	Owl Head Charm Pencil, 1¾ inches	1.80
16024	Black Cat Head Charm Pencil, 1¾ inches	1.80
16018	Frog Head Charm Pencil, 1¾ inches	1.80

The above four numbers are very attractive and useful watch chain favor charms.

HALLOWE'EN FORTUNE TELLING SETS

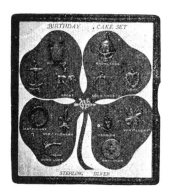

16/52

32/118

		DOZEN SETS
32/91	Fortune Telling Cake Sets, containing 8 Assorted Favors	$ .80
32/118	Fortune Telling Cake Sets, containing 15 Good Assorted Favors	2.25
16/50	Fortune Telling Cake Sets, containing 5 Sterling Silver Favors	3.60
16/51	Fortune Telling Cake Sets, containing 8 Sterling Silver Favors	4.80
16/52	Fortune Telling Cake Sets, containing 12 Sterling Silver Favors	6.25

The above five numbers are neatly boxed, containing Favors with description indicating the meaning of each article.

These are wonderful all-year-'round selling items.

		DOZEN
32/105	Fortune Telling Wheel, with 12 small fortune telling pumpkins on attractive lithographed card, 14¼ inches, each in envelope	$.75
32/67	Pumpkin Game, with 24 numbers to be stuck on eye, Donkey Party style, 27 inches	.80
31/602	Revelation Fortune Telling Cards, full deck of gilt-edged cards with instructions	7.20
32/274	"Zhorai" Fortune Telling Game, 52 different fortunes in attractive Hallowe'en design box, 5 inches, quite new	1.10
32/400	"Dippy Dips," the game with a hundred stunts, each player punches board for instructions, 3 x 4½ inches	3.60

14

HALLOWE'EN PAPER HATS AND MASKS

117

34/309

32/104

34/1H

15

DRESSED HALLOWE'EN KEWPIE DOLLS

10/24

80/9

		DOZEN
10/9	Celluloid Kewpie Pumpkin, with pumpkin head and stem, 2½ inches....	$2.00
10/24	Celluloid Kewpie Witch, with hat and cape trimmed with orange color ribbon, 2½ inches	2.00
10/18	Celluloid Kewpie Devil, dressed in red with hood and horns, 2½ inches	2.00
10/103	Celluloid Kewpie Hallowe'en Girl, with large orange hat and black plume, 2½ inches	2.00
10/104	Celluloid Kewpie Hallowe'en Girl with sunbonnet and skirt, 2½ inches	2.00
10/136	Celluloid Kewpie Hallowe'en Party Girl, dressed in carnival costume, 2½ inches	2.00
10/142	Celluloid Kewpie Hallowe'en Clown Boy, dressed in orange and black, 2½ inches	2.00
10/119	Celluloid Kewpie Hallowe'en Sport Girl, dressed in orange and black hat and sporty dress. 2½ inches................................	2.00
10/109	Celluloid Kewpie Farmer Boy Holding Pumpkin, 2½ inches................	2.00

IF SO DESIRED WE CAN SUPPLY DRESSED DOLLS IN ALL OF THE ABOVE STYLES AT $1.50 PER DOZ.

LARGER DRESSED CELLULOID KEWPIES

This is a very popular size.

		DOZEN
80/9	Celluloid Kewpie Pumpkin, with pumpkin head, stem and trimmings, 3½ inches	$3.60
80/24	Celluloid Kewpie Witch, with hat, cape and broom, 3½ inches..............	3.60
80/105	Celluloid Kewpie Hallowe'en Tam O'Shanter Girl, with orange dress and pumpkin cutout in hand, 3½ inches................................	4.20
80/117	Celluloid Kewpie Miss Hallowe'en, with fancy trimmed hat, orange and green dress, holding pumpkin cutout, 3½ inches............................	4.20
80/142	Hallowe'en Clown Boy, with black mask and orange color clown hat, 3½ inches	4.20
80/10	Celluloid Kewpie Cook, holding spoon, 3½ inches	4.20
80/109	Celluloid Kewpie Farmer Boy with cap and green trousers, holding pumpkin, 3½ inches	4.20

All of the above Kewpie Dolls are mounted on heavy white glazed round bases.

IF SO DESIRED WE CAN SUPPLY DRESSED DOLLS IN ALL OF THE ABOVE STYLES AT $2.25 DOZ.

55/146   34/319

CHINA KEWPIES DRESSED IN ATTRACTIVE HALLOWE'EN STYLES

		DOZEN
55/109	China Kewpie Pumpkin, with Pumpkin Head, Stem and Trimmings, 4¾ inches	$5.40
55/124	China Kewpie Witch, with Cape and Black Hat,˙ Holding Broom, 4¾ inches	5.40
55/115	China Kewpie Hallowe'en Girl, Dressed in Artistic Orange Dress and Shirred Hat; Holding Pumpkin Cutout, 4¾ inches	7.20
55/146	China Kewpie Hallowe'en "Mildred," Dressed in Artistic Orange Dress and Trimmed Maline Hat, 4¾ inches	7.80
55/103	China Kewpie Hallowe'en American Beauty, Dressed Elaborately in Various Styles for Hallowe'en in Silks and Malines, 4¾ inches.	10.20
103/6	China Kewpie. Dressed in Fluffy Orange Color Maline Skirt, Satin Hat and Holding Shower of Pumpkin Cutouts, 8½ inches. Beautiful Show or Window Piece	33.00

HALLOWE'EN KEWPIES ON ROUND ORANGE COLOR BOX

		DOZEN
93/205	China Kewpie Doll, Dressed as Hallowe'en Girl in Orange and Black Crepe Paper, with Pumpkin Lantern in Hand, Mounted on Orange and Black Decorated 3 inch Round Box	$9.00
93/206	China Kewpie Doll, Dressed as Devil with Pitchfork in Hand, Mounted on Red Decorated 3 Inch Round Box	9.00
93/2070	China Kewpie Doll, Dressed as Black Cat, with Orange Bow Around Collar, Mounted on 3 Inch Round Box	9.00

HALLOWE'EN DECORATIONS, GARLANDS, CUTOUTS, ETC.

		GROSS
34/340	Orange and Black Folding Garland, Oblong Shaped, 1¾x2¼ inches, 6 feet long.	$3.00
34/339	Orange and Black Folding Garland, 3x4 inches, 10 feet long	3.90
34/319	Orange and Black Folding Garlands, with Five Pumpkin Heads, 3½ inches wide, 10 feet long	8.70
34/311	Hallowe'en Garlands, Witch, Cat, Owl and Pumpkin Cutouts, 5½ feet long.	9.00
F927/25/1	Orange Colored Tissue Paper Garland with Comic Cutouts, 6 feet long.	7.80
F947/25/3	Orange and Black Tissue Paper Garland, 6 feet long	12.00

17

HALLOWE'EN CUTOUTS

34/351   34/313

		GROSS
34/313	Dancing Skeleton, Cardboard, Jointed Arms and Legs, 24 inches, suspended from string	$9.25
34/314	Wriggling Snake, Cardboard, 36 inches, suspended from string	4.80
34/338	Johnny Pumpkin Head, Cardboard Pumpkin Figure with Movable Head, Holding Black Cat, 19 inches	8.40
34/345	Cardboard Witch Figure, with Movable Arms and Legs, Highly Colored, 18 inches.	9.00
34/344	Cardboard Pumpkin Figures with Movable Arms and Legs, Highly Colored, 21 inches.	9.25
34/346	Pumpkin Face Clock with Movable Hands and Pumpkin Shaped Pendulum, 14 inches.	9.00
34/351	Cardboard Black Cat with Movable Legs, Tail and Head, 15 inches.	9.00

		DOZEN ENVELOPES
34/347	Comic Hallowe'en Imitation Cards, 5 Assorted Styles to Envelope, 5 inches.	$.40
34/343	Black Cat Silhouettes, 10 Cutouts in Envelopes, 3½ inches	.55
34/348	Standing Comic Pumpkin Figure, Highly Decorated, 5 in Envelopes, 5 inches.	.40
34/312	Black Cardboard Silhouettes, 5 Assorted Styles in Envelope, 8 inches.	.70

		DOZEN
H78	Cardboard Witch Riding Broom, Silhouette, 7 inches	$.40
H69	Giant Black Cat Silhouette, 12 inches	.70

		GROSS
16723	Pressed Paper Skull and Crossed Bones, 1½ inches	$2.70
16718	Pressed Paper Pumpkin Face, 1½ inches	2.40
16722	Pressed Paper Black Witch Cat, 2½ inches	2.40
16724	Three Red Devils Sitting on Broom, 3 inches	2.40

The last four items are well made and artistically colored.

HALLOWE'EN SEALS, NAPKINS, ETC.

		DOZEN BOXES
H585	Witch and Broom Seal, 1 inch, 25 in box	$.80
H583	Black Witch Cat Seal, 1 inch, 25 in box	.80
H641	Pumpkin Seal, 1 inch, 25 in box	.80
H275	Hallowe'en Table Cover, 63x84 inches ....per doz.	$2.80
H822	Hallowe'en Crepe Paper Napkins ....per 1000	3.00

		PER 100
H835	Hallowe'en Crepe Paper Folds for Decorating	$10.00

		DOZEN ENVELOPES
34/349	Tally Card, 5 Assorted Designs with Extra Scoring Pad, in Attractive Envelope.	$.55
34/342	Place Cards, 10 Assorted Designs in Attractive Envelopes	.55
34/347	Hallowe'en Invitations, 5 Assorted Styles in Attractive Envelopes....	.55

		PER 100
32/149	Cute Hallowe'en Girl, with Black Cat Place Cards	$2.00
32/150	Comic Pumpkin and Black Cats Place Cards	1.50
32/151	Hallowe'en Girl with Fortune Teller Place Cards	2.50
32/363	Hallowe'en Greeting Card with Pumpkin Face and Miniature Glass Whisky Flask, each in envelope	5.25

HALLOWE'EN SNAPPING MOTTOES

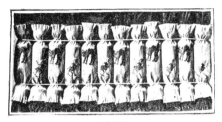

94/46

55/132	Orange Crepe Paper Motto, with Witch Cutout, 12 to the box, each motto 6 inches.	**GROSS** $3.90
55/130	Orange Crepe Paper Motto, with Black Cat Picture, 12 to the box, each motto 6½ inches.	4.20
55/131	Orange Crepe Paper Motto,, with Assorted Hallowe'en Cutouts, 12 to the box, each motto 8½ inches	4.20
55/133	Orange Crepe Paper Motto, with Black Cat Picture, 12 to the box, each motto 9½ inches.	7.20
55/134	Orange Crepe Paper Motto, with Witch Cutouts and Double Fringed Ends, 12 to the box, each motto 8½ inches	6.60
Sweety H	Orange Crepe Paper Motto, with Black Cat and Fringed Ends. 8	4.35
268	Orange Crepe Paper Tissue Mottoes, with Fringed Ends and Black Cat, 8½ inches.	5.40

Each motto contains a hat, favor, snapper and verse, except the last two numbers, which contain snapper and imported cap only.

THE "ELSCO" SNAPPING MOTTOES

DESIGNED and MANUFACTURED by us in our own FACTORY containing LARGE HATS, GOOD TOYS, MOTTO VERSE and SNAPPER. We use DENNISON'S BEST CREPE ONLY. Packed in strong WHITE GLAZED BOXES. A REAL AMERICAN PRODUCT.

94/50	Orange and Black Combination Motto, with Pressed Paper Pumpkin Head, packed 12 to the box, each motto 8½ inches	**GROSS** $8.40
94/283	Pumpkin Orange Color Motto, with Black Witch Cat Cutout, 12 to the box, each motto 8½ inches	9.60
94/282	Pumpkin Orange Color Motto, with Black Witch Cutout, 12 to the box, each motto 8½ inches	9.60
94/284X	Orange and Black Crepe Paper Motto, with Black Owl Cutout, 12 to the box, each motto 8½ inches	9.60
94/286	Orange Crepe Paper Motto, with Skull Head Cutout, 12 to the box, each motto 8½ inches.	10.20
94/46	Pumpkin Orange Color Motto, with Black and Orange Double Ruffle Ends, Decorated with Skull, Devil and Black Cat, 12 to the box, each motto 8½ inches.	12.00
94/56	Pumpkin Color Motto, with Double Ends Decorated with Comic Pumpkin Heads, 12 to the box, each motto 8½ inches	15.00

LARGE HALLOWE'EN SNAPPING MOTTOES

		DOZEN BOXES
94/61	Large Pumpkin Color Motto, with Orange and Black Crimped Ends, Decorated with Black Cutouts, 6 to the box, each motto 13	$12.00
94/60	Large Pumpkin Color Motto, with Orange and Black Crimped Ends, Decorated with Skull, Black Cat and Flowers, 6 to the box, each motto 13 inches.	14.40
94/59	Large Pumpkin Color Motto, with Orange and Black Fringed Ends, Decorated with Pumpkin Faced Peanut Shell, 6 to the box, each motto 13 inches.	14.40
94/58	Large Pumpkin Color Motto, with Orange and Black Crimped Ends, Decorated with Autumn Leaves and Pumpkin Cutouts, 6 to the box, each motto 13 inches	14.40
94/294	Large Orange and Black Motto Rose Petal Design, Ends Decorated with Red Devils, 6 to the box, each motto 13 inches	15.60

THE "*ELSCO*" HALLOWE'EN JACK HORNER PIES

Are CREATED by an EXPERT ARTIST and MANUFACTURED in our own
FACTORY. Most ORIGINAL and DISTINCTIVE containing SPLENDID
FAVORS for all occasions. DENNISON'S BEST CREPE only used.

355/35	92/203	93/200

		EACH
92/250	Tulip Shaped Jack Horner Pie in Orange and Green Crepe, 9 inches high, 7 inches diameter, 6 ribbons	$1.50
92/201	Pumpkin Shaped Jack Horner Pie with Stem, Natural Color, 15 inches diameter, with 12 ribbons, $3.00; with black caton top	3.50
92/203	Witch Kettle Tripod, Decorated with Witch and Cat Cutouts, Large Chiffon Bow on Top, 22 inches high, 12 ribbons	4.00
92/207	Pumpkin Figure Jack Horner Pie, with Comic Hat Carrying Favors, 20 inches high, 15 inches wide, 12 ribbons	4.50
92/265	Comic Face Hallowe'en Clock Jack Horner Pie, Decorated with Black Cat and Witch Cutouts, 15 inches high, 12 ribbons	4.50
92/267	Clown Figure Jack Horner Pie in Orange and Black Crepe Paper, Decorated with Silver Bells, Very Artistic and Effective, 20 inches high	6.00

HALLOWE'EN NUT CUPS

		GROSS
42/10011	Round Crepe Paper Hallowe'en Color Nut Cup	$3.60
40/717	Oval Orange and Black Crepe Paper Basket with Rope Handle	4.20
42/65	Pumpkin Color Comic Candlestick Shape Case with Black Handle	4.80
42/67	Pumpkin Color Round Case with Black Cat Decoration	4.80
40/718	Orange and Black Sunflower Case with Rope Handle, Very Attractive	6.60

		PER 100
355/35	Round Crepe Paper Orange Color Case with Black Witch Cutout	$3.75
355/37	Orange and Black Combination Crepe Paper Basket with Rope Handle	4.00
355/102	Orange and Black Combination Case with Witch and Black Cat Cutout	4.00
355/96	Orange and Black Combination Covered Box with Black Cat Cutout	5.00
355/92	Pumpkin Color Case, on Wheels with Black Cat	5.50
355/104	Orange Color Crepe Paper Basket with Black Cat Ribbon on Wire Handle	5.50
355/36	Round Pumpkin Color Basket with Black Cat and Ribbon Bow on Handle	7.50
355/40	Round Pumpkin Color Basket with Comic Face Pumpkin on Handle	9.00
93/237	Round Orange Crepe Covered Basket with Comic Witch Picture	6.50
93/236	Round Orange Crepe Covered Basket with Red Devil Figure	12.00
93/232	Orange Crepe Covered Box with Owl Picture	16.00
93/200	Orange Color Round Box with Comic Pumpkin and Clown Hat, 9½ inches	20.00

**$25.00, $50.00, $75.00 and $100.00 Hallowe'en Assortments are given our special
attention and we are sure will prove most satisfactory.**

20

THANKSGIVING NOVELTIES
TURKEYS

641/225   641/228

High grade imported Turkeys well made and artistically painted.

		GROSS
4007	Turkey Gobbler, 2 inches	$6.90
18765	Turkey Gobbler with Wire Legs on Round Base, 1¾ inches	7.20
431/120	Turkey Gobbler, 1½ inches	7.80
9805	Miniature Turkey Gobbler on Base, 1½ inches	8.40
641/222	Turkey Gobbler, 2¼ inches.	9.00
4008	Turkey Gobbler, 3 inches.	9.60
641/115	Turkey Hen, Assorted Positions, 2¼ inches	11.40
641/116	Turkey Hen, Assorted Positions, 3 inches	15.00

		DOZEN
10884	Turkey Gobbler, Nicely Painted, 3 inches	$1.05
10895	Turkey Gobbler, 3½ inches.	1.35
19300	Turkey Gobbler Box, 3¼ inches.	1.70
641/232	Turkey Gobbler Box, 4½ inches.	2.20
641/231	Turkey Gobbler Box, 4½ inches	2.40
307/940	Turkey Gobbler Box, 4¾ inches	2.70
641/224	Turkey Gobbler Box, 5½ inches	3.75
641/225	Turkey Gobbler Box, 6¾ inches	7.80
641/122	Turkey Gobbler Box, 9 inches	14.40
725/151	Turkey Gobbler Box, 10¾ inches	23.40
725/152	Turkey Gobbler Box, 11¾ inches	27.00
725/153	Turkey Gobbler Box, 13½ inches	39.00
725/161	Turkey Hen Box, 5¾ inches	5.25
641/228	Turkey Hen Box, 6 inches	5.70
725/162	Turkey Hen Box, 7 inches	7.20
27161	Turkey Hen Box, 10 inches	39.00
25109	Comic Turkey Gobbler on Base with Removable Head for Filling, 4½ inches.	1.60
725/186	Turkey Gobbler Standing on Tree Log (Box), 3½ inches	1.40
725/187	Turkey Hen Standing on Tree Log (Box), 3½ inches	1.10
14895	Celluloid Standing Turkey Gobbler with Place Card Holder, Well Painted, 2½ inches.	1.65

Lower Priced Turkeys of Cheaper Quality

		GROSS
641/113	Turkey Gobbler, 1¾ inches.	$4.20
27144	Turkey Gobbler, 2½ inches.	6.60
27145	Turkey Gobbler (Box), 3½ inches	9.00
27146	Turkey Gobbler (Box), 4¼ inches	15.00
641/226	Turkey Gobbler on Rustic Log (Box), 3½ inches	7.20
27141	Turkey Gobbler with Shaking Head, 2½ inches	8.40
725/196	Turkey Gobbler with Shaking Head on Round Box, 3 inches	10.20
725/197	Turkey Gobbler with Shaking Head on Round Box, 3½ inches	15.60

THANKSGIVING NOVELTIES (Continued)
ROAST TURKEYS

		DOZEN
307/630	Roast Turkey (Box), Cheaper Quality, 3 inches	$.65
5000	Roast Turkey (Box), Best Quality, 3 inches	.80
5001	Roast Turkey (Box), Best Quality, 3¾ inches	1.60
5002	Roast Turkey (Box), Best Quality, 4½ inches	2.00
5003	Roast Turkey (Box), Best Quality, 6 inches	3.60
5004	Roast Turkey (Box), Best Quality, 7 inches	4.50
5005	Roast Turkey (Box), Best Quality, 8 inches	6.00
5006	Roast Turkey (Box), Best Quality, 9 inches	7.20
5007	Roast Turkey (Box), Best Quality, 10 inches	10.20

FRUIT BASKETS

		DOZEN
12104	Miniature Straw Basket Filled with Fruit, 2½ inches	.70
12100	Round Open Straw Basket Filled with Fruit, 2 inches	.70
12101	Oval Shape Straw Basket with Two Handles, Filled with Fruit, 3 inches.	1.00
11846	Straw Basket with Fruit on Lid which can be removed, 3 inches	1.10
11876	Straw Basket with Fruit on Lid which can be removed, 5 inches	3.50
11878	Straw Basket with Fruit on Lid which can be removed, 6 inches	4.80
11877	Straw Basket with Fruit on Lid which can be removed, 7 inches	6.00
11880	Straw Basket with Fruit on Lid which can be removed, 8½ inches	10.00

The last four items are well made of painted plaited straw and
make very attractive Candy containers.

7302/62	355/43	5002

		DOZEN
60/103/1	Miniature Roast Turkey on Silver Plate, 3 inches	$.38
68/45	Celluloid Plates with Assorted Eatables, 3½ inches	1.20
355/43	Imitation Wood Butcher's Block with Turkey Gobbler and Cleaver, 6 inches.	2.40
7302/62	Cook Figure Carrying Roast Turkey on Plate (Box), 3 inches	1.35
12747/125	Miniature Knitted Doll Cook Figure, 2 inches	.85
33/121	Comic Thanksgiving Child Figures on Box, 4 inches	.85
355/101	Pumpkin Color Square Box with Turkey Gobbler, 2 inches	.50
27077	Comic Vegetable Figures with Shaking Arms and Legs, 1½ inches	.40
520/177	Comic Pumpkin Figures with Shaking Arms and Legs, 2½ inches	.35
27143	Comic Turkey Gobbler Standing with Open Pumpkin, 4 inches	1.70
16748	Pressed Paper Roast Turkey, Well Painted, 3 inches	.55
5541	Miniature Roast Turkey, Well Made, 1½ inches	.75
566/921	Celluloid Figures with Assorted Vegetable Heads, 3½ inches	.45
12919	Miniature Frying Pan with Handle, 4 inches	.42
15000	Miniature Metal Roasting Pan with Two Handles, 3½ inches	.60
15001	Miniature Metal Roasting Pan with Two Handles, 4½ inches	.85
16780	Pressed Paper Turkey Gobbler on Box, 4 inches	.85
16781	Pressed Paper Turkey Gobbler on Box, 5½ inches	1.45

THANKSGIVING NOVELTIES (Continued)

		DOZEN
9806	Assorted Hens and Roosters with Metal Feet, 2½ inches......................	$.85
9807	Assorted Geese and Ducks with Metal Feet, 3 inches............................	.85
		GROSS
14303	Pressed Paper Turkey Gobbler with Snapper and Favor, 2½ inches....	$4.80
14323	Pressed Paper Roast Turkey with Snapper and Favor, 3 inches............	4.80
27160	Wax Pumpkin Box, 1½ inches...	4.20
27050	Wax Pumpkin Box, 2½ inches...	9.00

5502   355/98

		DOZEN
34421	Wax Fruits, Assorted Apple, Pear, Orange and Lemon, 6 to box, 3 inches.	$.60
5023	Wax Bananas (Box), 6 inches..	1.35
4029	Silk Covered Apple with Green Leaf, 2 inches....................................	.80
15711	Pressed Paper Apple (Box), 2½ inches..	.35
15709	Pressed Paper Pear (Box), 2½ inches..	.35
15700	Pressed Paper Peanut (Box), 3 inches...	.32
15701	Pressed Paper Peanut (Box), 5 inches...	.42
15702	Pressed Paper Walnut (Box), 2½ inches..	.35
5022	Wax Pear (Box), Well Made, 3 inches...	1.50
5021	Wax Apple (Box), Well Made, 2½ inches...	1.50
5017	Wax Orange (Box), Well Made, 2½ inches...	2.00

MINIATURE PLATES OF EATABLES

		DOZEN
12915	Paper Plate with Assorted Cakes, 1½ inches......................................	$.30
5508	Paper Plate with Assorted Fruit, 2 inches..	.40
5514	Paper Plate with Assorted Cakes, 2½ inches......................................	.75
32/80	Paper Plate with Assorted Fruits, 3 inches...	.38
5547	Metal Frying Pan with Sausages and Eggs...	.65
5517	Metal Frying Pan with Sausages and Eggs...	1.00
5502	Frankfurter with Roll and Sauerkraut, 3 inches.................................	2.05

THANKSGIVING SNAPPING MOTTOES

Each Motto Contains a Hat, Snapper, Favor and Verse

		GROSS
55/137	Pumpkin Color Motto with Turkey Picture, 12 to the box, each motto 8 inches.	$3.90
55/138	Pumpkin Color Motto, with Turkey Standing on Pumpkin, 12 to the box, each motto 8½ inches..	6.60

THE "ELSCO" SNAPPING MOTTOES

		GROSS
94/55	Pumpkin Color Motto, with Pressed Paper Turkey Gobbler and Crimped Ends, 12 to the box, each motto 8½ inches....................	$9.60
94/54	Pumpkin Color Motto, with Crimped Ends Decorated with Autumn Leaves, 12 to the box, each motto 8½ inches............................	9.60
94/92	Pumpkin Color Motto with Double Crimped Ends, Decorated with Pressed Paper Turkey Gobbler, 12 to the box, each motto 8½ inches.	10.20

		DOZEN BOXES
94/65	Large Pumpkin Color Motto, with Crimped Ends, Decorated with Ribbons and Autumn Leaves, 6 to the box, each motto 13 inches.	$14.40
94/64	Large Pumpkin Color Motto, with Orange and Green Fringe Ends, Decorated with Bunches of Grapes and Autumn Leaves, 6 to the box, each motto 13 inches...	15.60

THANKSGIVING NOVELTIES (Continued)
THANKSGIVING PLACE AND TALLY CARDS

		PER 100
32/152	Turkey Gobbler, Lithographed, with Extra Piece for Scoring..............	$1.65
32/153	Turkey Gobbler, Nicely Lithographed............................	1.20
32/154	Children with Turkey Gobbler....................	2.00

THANKSGIVING SEALS

		DOZEN BOXES
T575	Turkey Gobbler Seal, 1 inch, 25 in box...............	$.80

TABLE COVERS, NAPKINS, ETC.

		DOZEN
T280	Thanksgiving Crepe Paper Table Covers, 68x84 inches...............	$2.80
		PER 1,000
T852	Thanksgiving Crepe Paper Napkins...................	$3.00
		PER 100
T856	Thanksgiving Folds Crepe Paper for Decorating...............	$10.00

THANKSGIVING JACK HORNER PIES

42/69   92/212

THE "ELSCO" JACK HORNER PIES

Are CREATED by an EXPERT ARTIST and MANUFACTURED in our own FACTORY. Most ORIGINAL and DISTINCTIVE containing SPLENDID FAVORS for all occasions. DENNISON'S BEST CREPE only used.

		EACH
93/236	Poppy Design Jack Horner Pie in Gold Color Crepe, 9 inches diameter, 7 inches high, 6 ribbons...............	$1.50
92/209	Large Pumpkin with Sprays of Assorted Grapes and Autumn Leaves, Large Turkey Gobbler, Standing on Top, 14 inches, 12 ribbons.	4.00
92/212	Haywagon Pie, Large Wagon Filled with Hay, Drawn by Two Cows, Farmer Kewpie Driver, Base of Pie, 12x24 inches, 12 ribbons.	5.50
92/213	Horn of Plenty Pie, Large Horn of Plenty Covered with Orange Color Rose Petals and Autumn Leaves, Filled with Apples, Grapes, etc., 27 inches, 12 ribbons...............	4.00
92/223	Chrysanthemum Pie, Pumpkin Shaped, Covered with Chrysanthemums and Autumn Leaves, Large Turkey Standing on Top, 14 inches, 12 ribbons.	6.00

THANKSGIVING NUT CUPS AND ICE CASES

		GROSS
42/70	Orange and Green Open Case with Turkey Seal....................	$4.50
42/69	Orange Basket with Turkey Seal, Two Handles....................	8.40
		PER 100
355/106	Orange and Green Nut Basket with Turkey on Handle....................	$4.00
355/108	Orange Basket with Turkey Cutout and Two Handles....................	5.25
355/93	Turkey Pulling Orange Colored Case on Wheels....................	5.25
355/98	Open Pumpkin Case with Green Leaf....................	6.25
91/210	Orange Color Open Case with Gold Turkey Cutout....................	7.50
355/105	Orange Color Basket with Miniature Apple on Handle....................	5.50
355/99	Round Orange Color Box with 3 Tiny Pumpkins....................	9.50
91/211	Orange Color Rose Basket with Fruits and Ribbon Bow on Handle....	17.00
355/97	Round Orange Color Box with Turkey Gobbler....................	21.00

24

THANKSGIVING DRESSED KEWPIE DOLLS

		DOZEN
10/10	Celluloid Kewpie Cook with White Apron and Cook's Hat, 2½ inches.	$2.00
10/11	Celluloid Kewpie Farmer with Brown Overalls, Hat and Whiskers, 2½ inches.	2.00
10/9	Celluloid Kewpie Pumpkin, with Pumpkin Head and Stem, 2½ inches.	2.00
10/147	Celluloid Kewpie Coming Out of Pumpkin, 2½ inches	2.00

If so desired, we can supply dressed dolls in all of the above styles at $1.50 per dozen.

		DOZEN
80/10	Celluloid Kewpie Thanksgiving Chef with White Apron, Cook's Hat and Spoon in Hand, 3½ inches	$4.20
80/11	Celluloid Kewpie Farmer with Brown Overalls, Hat and Whiskers, Holding Pumpkin, 3½ inches	4.20
80/9	Celluloid Kewpie Pumpkin with Pumpkin Head, Stem and Trimmings, 3½ inches.	3.60
80/120	Celluloid Kewpie Thanksgiving Girl Dressed in Orange and Green Fringed Skirt and Hat, Holding Comic Pumpkin Figure, 3½ inches.	4.20
55/10	China Kewpie Thanksgiving Chef with White Apron, Cook's Hat and Pan in Hand, 4¾ inches.	6.00
55/11	China Kewpie Farmer with Rake and Pumpkin, 4¾ inches	6.60
93/215	China Kewpie Doll Dressed in Gold Color Crepe Paper and Fancy Hat Trimmed with Chiffon Bow, Carrying Basket of Fruit, Mounted on 3-inch Round Box	9.00
93/216	China Kewpie Doll Dressed in Gold and Green Color Crepe Paper, Small Turkey Seal in Hand, Mounted on 3-inch Box	9.00

$25.00, $50.00, $75.00 THANKSGIVING Assortments Are Given Our Special Attention and We Are Sure Will Prove Most Satisfactory.

FOOTBALL FAVORS

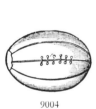 

9004	10/77	725/100

		DOZEN
9003	Football, Imitation Leather, 1½ inches	$.70
9004	Football, Imitation Leather, 2¼ inches	1.10
9005	Football, Imitation Leather, 4¼ inches	1.40
9086	Football, Imitation Leather, 5½ inches	2.20
9082	Football, Imitation Leather, 6 inches	3.00
9083	Football, Imitation Leather, 7½ inches	4.80

The above items are perfect imitations and can be filled.

		GROSS
725/100	Miniature Football on Pin, 2 inches	$4.50
15707	Football Box, Cheaper Quality, 2½ inches	3.00
2445/124	Football Box, Tin, 2 inches	3.90

KEWPIE FOOTBALL PLAYERS

		DOZEN
10/77	Celluloid Kewpie Football Player with Painted Sweater, Tan Trousers and Cap, Holding Football in Hand, 2½ inches	$2.00
80/77	Celluloid Kewpie Football Player with Painted Sweater, Tan Trousers, and Cap, Holding Football in Hand, 3½ inches	4.20
55/77	China Kewpie Football Player, same as 80/77 but 4¾ inches	6.60

The above three numbers can be had in suitable colors and lettering for all colleges.

25

CHRISTMAS NOVELTIES

1289/8   10812

		DOZEN
4015	Red Coat Santa Claus with Tree, 4 inches	$.42
4016	Red Coat Santa Claus with Tree, 6½ inches	.75
4017	Red Coat Santa Claus with Basket on Back, 4½ inches	.75
4018	Red Coat Santa Claus with Basket on Back, 7 inches	1.20
4019	Red Coat Santa Claus with Basket on Back, 9 inches	2.10
4020	Red Coat Santa Claus with White Fur Trimming and Tree, 9½ inches.	4.00
4021	Red Coat Santa Claus with White Fur Trimming and Tree, 10½ in.....	6.30
18774	Red Paper Mache Santa Claus, 3 inches	.30
34420	Red Paper Mache Santa Claus with Shaking Head, 3¼ inches	.60
9816	Red Paper Mache Santa Claus Box, 4½ inches	.60
9713	Red Painted Santa Claus Box, 5 inches	1.00
9823	Painted Santa Claus Figure on Wire Spring, 2 inches	.75
9824	Painted Santa Claus Figure with Shaking Head on Box, 3¾ inches.....	.85
24803	Painted Santa Claus Figure on Round Box, 3½ inches	.80
24804	Painted Santa Claus Figure on Round Box, 4½ inches	1.35
1289	Painted Santa Claus Figure on Glistening Snowball, Box, 4 inches......	1.40

SANTA CLAUS FIGURES WITH PAINTED BLUE TROUSERS AND WHITE FUR BEARD

		DOZEN
1289/7	Santa Claus (Box), 7 inches	$3.40
1289/8	Santa Claus (Box), 8 inches	5.80
1289/9	Santa Claus (Box), 10 inches	8.70
1289/10	Santa Claus (Box), 12 inches	12.60

SANTA CLAUS FIGURES WITH BLUE CLOTH TROUSERS AND WHITE FUR BEARD

		DOZEN
1289/11	Santa Claus (Box), 8 inches	$3.90
1289/12	Santa Claus (Box), 9 inches	6.90
1289/13	Santa Claus (Box), 10 inches	9.80
1289/14	Santa Claus (Box), 12 inches	15.30
1289/15	Santa Claus (Box), 14 inches	22.80
1289/16	Santa Claus (Box), 18 inches	42.00
1289/17	Santa Claus (Box), 26 inches	93.00

SANTA CLAUS FIGURES WITH BLUE CLOTH TROUSERS AND WHITE FUR BEARD, STOOPING POSITION CARRYING SACK ON BACK

		DOZEN
10812	Santa Claus, 8 inches	$7.20
10813	Santa Claus, 9½ inches	9.60
10814	Santa Claus, 14 inches	21.00

SANTA CLAUS FIGURE WITH MECHANICAL MUSIC BOX

		EACH
1289/21	Santa Claus Figure, Box, with Long Red Coat, White Fur Beard. Has Mechanical Music Box which Plays Christmas Carols, 22 inches.	$8.00

CHRISTMAS NOVELTIES (Continued)

China Face Santa Claus Figures, with Beautifully Colored Cotton and Crepe Paper Suit and Hat. Our Own Exclusive Importation

60/1037

6005

		DOZEN
6025	Santa Claus Figure Sitting on Square Box, 4½ inches...........................	$1.95
6023	Santa Claus Figure with Paper Basket on Back, 7 inches......................	3.50
6026	Santa Claus Figure Sitting on Tree Stump and Logs, Assorted, 7 in..	3.60
6005	Santa Claus Figure, Standing Position Box, 7½ inches......................	3.70
6011	Santa Claus Figure, Standing Position Box, 9½ inches......................	6.00
6024	Santa Claus Figure, Standing Position with Basket Container on Back, 9½ inches.	5.40
6028	Santa Claus Figure Sitting on Tree Log and Stump, Assorted (Box), 10½ inches.	8.70
6030	Large Santa Claus Figure Sitting on Tree Stump and Log, Assorted (Box), 21 inches.	36.00
6036	Santa Claus Figure Sitting on White Wood Sled with Nicely Decorated Sack Container, 6½ inches.....................	5.40
6037	Same as 6036 but size, 9¼ inches.....................	10.20
6038	Same as 6036 but size, 10¼ inches.....................	13.20
60/1037	Santa Claus with Red Cloth Coat, Pulling Open Wooden Sled, Mounted on Frosted Wood Base, 17 inches.....................	14.40
10912	Santa Claus with Red Cloth Coat Pulling Open Wood Sled, Mounted on Polished Wood Base, 15 inches.....................	15.00
10913	Same as 10912 but size, 20 inches.....................	21.60

RED COTTON SANTA CLAUS FIGURES

		GROSS
520/106	Red Cotton Santa Claus, 2¼ inches.....................	$1.50
520/107	Red Cotton Santa Claus, 4 inches.....................	3.00
520/108	Red Cotton Santa Claus, 6 inches.....................	4.80
520/109	Red Cotton Santa Claus on Snowball, 3 inches.....................	5.40

		DOZEN
355/540	Red Cotton Santa Claus Figure (Box), 8½ inches.....................	$2.10
60/1035	Jointed Santa Claus with Red Cloth Coat and Blue Cloth Trousers, 8 inches.	3.60
60/1036	Jointed Santa Claus with Red Cloth Coat and Blue Cloth Trousers, 11 inches.	6.90

CELLULOID SANTA CLAUS FIGURES

Well made of heavy celluloid and beautifully colored.

		DOZEN
35/151	Celluloid Santa Claus Figure with Bag of Toys, 4¼ inches.....................	$1.50
35/152	Celluloid Santa Claus Figure with Bag of Toys, 5¾ inches.....................	1.90
35/153	Celluloid Santa Claus Figure with Bag of Toys, 7½ inches.....................	3.50
35/154	Celluloid Santa Claus Figure with Bag of Toys, 9½ inches.....................	8.00

CHRISTMAS NOVELTIES (Continued)
SANTA CLAUS FIGURES ON RED CHIMNEY BOX

1289/2	9827	6028

		DOZEN
1289/1	Santa Claus, with Red Cloth Coat and White Fur Beard, Coming Out of Chimney (Box), 4 inches......	$2.35
1289/2	Santa Claus with Red Cloth Coat and White Fur Beard, Coming Out of Chimney (Box), 5½ inches......	4.25
1289/3	Santa Claus with Red Cloth Coat and White Fur Beard, Coming Out of Chimney (Box), 6½ inches......	6.90
1289/4	Santa Claus with Red Cloth Coat and White Fur Beard, Coming Out of Chimney (Box), 7½ inches......	9.60
1289/5	Santa Claus with Red Cloth Coat and White Fur Beard, Coming Out of Chimney (Box), 11 inches......	19.80
1289/6	Santa Claus with Red Cloth Coat and White Fur Beard, Coming Out of Chimney (Box), 13 inches......	35.40

All the above are well made of heavy cardboard covered with red imitation brick paper and the box containers have a paper lace edge. A most distinctive Novelty Candy Box.

		DOZEN
24799	Santa Claus, with Red Cloth Coat and White Beard, Coming Out of Chimney (Box), Cheaper Quality, 4½ inches......	$1.80
24800	Same as 24799 but size, 6 inches......	2.50
24801	Same as 24799 but size, 8¾ inches......	5.20
24802	Same as 24799 but size, 10½ inches......	8.40
9826	Santa Claus with Red Cloth Coat and White Fur Beard Sitting on Pile of Logs (Box), 5 inches......	1.90
9827	Santa Claus with Red Cloth Coat and White Fur Beard Sitting on Pile of Logs (Box), 6 inches......	3.60
9828	Santa Claus with Red Cloth Coat and White Fur Beard Sitting on Pile of Logs (Box), 7 inches......	5.40
60/1014	Santa Claus Sitting on Rustic Log (Box), 3 inches......	.70
9832	Santa Claus with Red Cloth Coat and White Fur Beard Sitting on Rustic Log (Box), 5 inches......	1.80
9833	Santa Claus with Red Cloth Coat and White Fur Beard Sitting on Rustic Log (Box), 6 inches......	3.70

CHRISTMAS NOVELTY BOXES

		DOZEN
16611/1	Round Cardboard Box, Assorted Bright Colors with Santa Claus Picture, 2¾ inches.	$.80
16611/2	Same as 16611/1 but size, 3¾ inches......	1.50
16611/2½	Same as 16611/1 but size, 4½ inches......	2.10
16611/3	Same as 16611/1 but size, 5¼ inches......	2.90
9184	Cardboard Basket Boxes, Assorted Shapes, Nicely Decorated, 3¼ inches......	1.10
5201/7	Cardboard Hat Boxes with Straps, Decorated with Poinsettias and Holly, 2½ inches.	1.30
5201/8	Cardboard Hat Boxes with Straps, Decorated with Poinsettias and Holly, 4 inches.	2.50
60/1031	Glistening Snow Baby on Round Box, Feeding Bird, 3½ inches......	1.60
725/309	White Glistening Snowball, Decorated with Holly (Box), 2¾ inches....	1.00
16492	Wooden Santa Claus Figure Pulling White Wood Sled Holding Decorated Cardboard Box, 11 inches......	5.40

CHRISTMAS NOVELTIES (Continued)
CHRISTMAS HOUSES (Containers)

| | 10877 | 4024 | 18605 |

		GROSS
4023	Christmas Houses, with Santa Claus, 6 Assorted Designs, 2½ inches..	$4.20
4024	Christmas Houses, with Santa Claus, 6 Assorted Designs, 3½ inches..	9.60
4025	Christmas Houses, with Santa Claus, 6 Assorted Designs, 4 inches......	10.00
4026	Christmas Houses, with Santa Claus and Christmas Tree, White Frosted Roof, 5 inches.	DOZEN $2.25
900/336	Cardboard Houses, Assorted Shapes with White Frosted Roof, 2½	.70
900/457	Cardboard Houses, Assorted Shapes with White Frosted Roof, 3½	1.00

COMIC CHRISTMAS NOVELTIES

10875	Comic Snow Child Sitting on Round Frosted Top Box, 2 inches.........	$.70
10876	Comic Snow Child Standing on Round Frosted Top Box, 3 inches.......	1.00
10877	Comic Snow Child Sitting on Pine Decorated Frosted Snowball Box, 3¼ inches.	1.10
10879	Comic Snow Child Nicely Colored on Skiis, 2½ inches...........................	1.10
10880	Comic Snow Child Nicely Colored Sitting on Frosted Sled, 1¾ inches.	.70
10881	Comic Snow Child Nicely Colored Sitting on Frosted Sled, 2¼ inches.	1.20
18658	White Glistening Snowman Figure with Painted Hat on Box, 4 inches.	.70
18609	Red Comic Santa (Box), 3½ inches...	.85
18605	White Glistening Snowman Figure with Black High Hat (Box), 5 inches.	1.10
17704	Comic Snowman Figure on Round Frosted Top Box, 3¾ inches.........	1.50
24806	Comic White Frosted Snowman Figure on Round Frosted Top Box, 4¾ inches.	1.40
24806	Comic Snowman Figure on Round White Frosted Box, 6½ inches....	2.25
12245/35	Santa Claus China Doll Figure with Brightly Colored Cricket Dress, 1¼ inches.	2.20
27005/2/1	Comic Santa Claus Doll Face Figure with White Beard and Nicely Colored Knitted Suit, 6 inches...............................	4.00
27005/2/2	Same as 27005/2/1 but size, 8½ inches..	7.80
19504	Santa Claus on Wire Spring, 2½ inches..	.35
18640	Red and White Frosted Christmas Open Basket with Handle, 3¾	.65
18640/2	White Frosted Christmas Open Basket with Handle and Red Decoration, 3 inches.	.65
33/122	Comic Winter Children on Box with Christmas Greetings, 5 inches......	.85
9029	Red Pressed Paper Sled (Box), 3 inches...	.80
1031/14	Comic Snowman Figure on Round Red Frosted Top Box, 5¼ inches.	1.20
19555	Comic Santa Claus Roly Poly on Wheels, 5 inches..............................	1.50
		PER 100
355/67	Red Sled Box Decorated with Holly Spray, 4½ inches........................	$8.00
355/68	Red Square Box Decorated with Holly Spray and Ribbon Bow, 3½	11.50
33/114	Suit Case Covered with Holly Paper, ¼ pound, 3½ inches....................	5.50

SANTA CLAUS MASKS

		DOZEN
32/187	Santa Claus Mask with Beard and Red Hood...............................	$2.25
32/368	Santa Claus Suit with Mask and Hood (Man Size)................................	36.00

29

CHRISTMAS NOVELTIES (Continued)
Juvenile China Face Figures with Attractively Colored Paper and Cotton Dresses Splendidly Made

1001   6000    1003   6001

		DOZEN
6017	Snow Children, Brightly Colored, Sitting Position, 2½ inches	$1.35
6000	Snow Children, Brightly Colored with Snowballs and Muffs, Assorted, 4 inches.	1.80
6020	Snow Children, Brightly Colored on Skiis, 4 inches	1.95
6022	Snow Children, Brightly Colored, Sitting on White Frosted Snowball, 3¾ inches.	2.05
6021	Snow Children, Brightly Colored, Sitting on White Frosted Top Box, 3¾ inches.	2.40
6001	Snow Children, Brightly Colored, Sitting on White Wood Sled and Skiis, Assorted, 4¼ inches.	2.05
6039	Snow Children, Brightly Colored, Sitting on Frosted Pine Branch, 6½ inches.	2.60
60/1010/1	White Cotton Glistening Snow Baby, Sitting on Wooden Sled (Box), 7 inches.	2.20
60/1011/1	White Cotton Glistening Snow Baby, Sitting on Wooden Sled (Box), 8½ inches.	3.75

CHINA SNOW FIGURES

		DOZEN
1000	White China Snow Babies, Assorted Positions, 1¼ inches	$.70
1001	White China Snow Babies on Skiis, 1½ inches	1.30
1002	White China Snow Babies, Sitting on Sled, 1½ inches	1.50
1003	White China Twin Snow Babies, Sitting on Sled, 2½ inches	2.40
1004	White China Snow Babies, Sitting on Sled, 3¼ inches	2.25
1005	White China Snow Babies, Lying on Sled, 3¼ inches	2.70
1006	White China Snow Babies, Assorted Positions, 3 inches	2.00
1039	White China Snow Babies, Sitting Position, 3½ inches	3.90
1042	White China Snow Babies on Skiis, Assorted Positions, 3½ inches	3.90
1038	Colored China Snow Babies with Movable Head, Sitting on White China Sled, 3¼ inches	2.70
1040	Colored China Twin Snow Babies, Sitting on Sled, 3¼ inches	3.90
1041	Colored China Twin Snow Babies, Movable Heads, Standing on Skiis, Mounted on China Base, 3½ inches	4.50
1046	China Father Christmas Snow Baby, 1¼ inches	1.40
1045	White China Christmas Doll with Movable Head, Nicely Decorated and Holding Christmas Tree	.90

CHRISTMAS NOVELTIES (Continued)
REINDEER

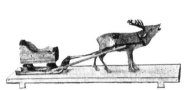

10804   10815

		DOZEN
10804	Papier Maché Reindeer, Natural Color (Box), 8½ inches	$4.90
10805	Papier Maché Reindeer, Natural Color (Box), 10½ inches	8.20
10806	Papier Maché Reindeer, Natural Color (Box), 13½ inches	16.80

METAL REINDEER

		DOZEN
2433/14	Metal Reindeer, Natural Color, Standing Position, 1½ inches	$.90
2433/37	Metal Reindeer, Natural Color, Standing Position, 3½ inches	1.65
45/500	Metal Reindeer, Natural Color, Standing Position, 2 inches	1.00
45/501	Metal Reindeer, Natural Color, Standing Position, 2¾ inches	1.45
45/502	Metal Reindeer, Natural Color, Standing Position, 4¼ inches	2.40
45/503	Metal Reindeer, Natural Color, Standing Position, 4¾ inches	3.00
45/504	Metal Reindeer, Natural Color, Standing Position, 6¾ inches	4.80

CELLULOID REINDEER

		DOZEN
35/155	Celluloid Reindeer, Natural Color, 3½ inches	$1.90
35/156	Celluloid Reindeer, Natural Color, 6 inches	4.00
35/157	Celluloid Reindeer, Natural Color, 9 inches	8.00

PRESSED PAPER REINDEER

		DOZEN
16703	Pressed Paper Reindeer, Natural Color, 2¼ inches	$.40
16701	Pressed Paper Reindeer, Natural Color, 2¾ inches	.75

REINDEER DRAWING SLED

		DOZEN
10815	One Reindeer, Natural Color, Drawing White Wood Sled Mounted on Frosted Base, 14 inches	$15.00
10816	Two Reindeer, Natural Color, Drawing White Wood Sled Mounted on Frosted Base, 17 inches	25.80
10817	Four Reindeer, Natural Color, Drawing White Wood Sled Mounted on Frosted Base, 28 inches	EACH 8.00

The last three numbers are very strong and beautifully made and are
very decorative window show pieces.

CHRISTMAS NOVELTIES (Continued)
FILLED CHRISTMAS STOCKINGS AND BAGS
The Ever Increasing Popular Form of Christmas Present for the Little Ones.

47/102   47/107

		GROSS
47/100	Filled Red Christmas Stockings, 10½ inches	$8.70
47/101	Filled Red Christmas Stockings, 12 inches	13.80
47/102	Filled Red Christmas Stockings, 15½ inches	22.80
		DOZEN
47/103	Filled Red Christmas Stockings, 18 inches	$3.85
47/104	Filled Red Christmas Stockings, 22 inches	8.40
47/105	Filled Red Christmas Stockings, 26 inches	16.80
		GROSS
47/106	Filled Red Christmas Bags with Handle, 6 inches	$9.25
		DOZEN
47/107	Filled Red Christmas Bags with Handle, 8 inches	$1.90
47/108	Filled Red Christmas Bags with Handle, 10 inches	3.85

**The above numbers are all made of Red Transparent Gauze
and well filled with Good Toys.**

IMPORTED REAL PINE BASKETS, SLEDS AND NOVELTY BOXES

		DOZEN
4970/1	Pine Wreaths Decorated with Holly Berries, 3½ inches	$1.00
4755	Pine Wreath Candle Holder, Decorated with Holly Berries and Pine Cones, 2 inches.	1.00
4765	Pine Cone Candle Holder, Decorated with Holly Berries and Pine Covered Handle, 2¼ inches	1.65
4976/2	Pine Cone Candle Holder, Decorated with Holly Berries and Pine Covered Handle, 4 inches	2.40
4976/3	Pine Cone Candle Holder, Decorated with Holly Berries and Pine Covered Handle, 5 inches	3.85
7500/2	Plaited Straw Basket with Two Handles, Decorated with Plain and Frosted Pine Cones and Branches, 5½ inches	3.75
7366/1	Pine Basket in Shape of Bird Nest, with Handle, Decorated with Pine Cones, Branches and Holly Berries, 6 inches	4.00
825/1	Round Basket with Hinged Cover, Decorated with Plain and Frosted Pine Branches, Cones and Holly Berries, Size 8 inches	10.20
6351/3	Open Plaited Straw Basket with Handle Made of Twisted Twigs, Decorated with Plain and Frosted Pine Cones and Branches, 10 inches.	7.20
7284	Round Plaited Twig Basket with Handle, Decorated with Plain and Frosted Pine Branches, Cones and Holly Berries, 18 inches	36.00
7520	Round Silvered Plaited Straw Basket with Handle, Decorated with Pine Branches and Clusters of Holly Berries and Leaves, 12½ inches.	12.60
4042/1	Frosted Pine Twig Sled, Decorated with Pine Branches and Cones, 8 inches.	3.90
7027/2	Frosted Pine Twig Sled, Decorated with Pine Branches and Cones, 12 inches.	12.60
11903	Oval or Round Plaited Twig Basket with Handle, Decorated with Holly Sprays or Mistletoe, 8 inches	3.80
11896	Oval Basket with Handle, Decorated with Pine Cones, Branches and Holly Berries, 9 inches	5.25

CHRISTMAS NOVELTIES (Continued)
FOLDING CHRISTMAS TREES

19910   5702   4013

		DOZEN
19902	Folding Christmas Tree, 16 inches	$1.25
19903	Folding Christmas Tree, 20 inches	2.10
19905	Folding Christmas Tree, 28 inches	7.20
19906	Folding Christmas Tree, 32 inches	9.60
19907	Folding Christmas Tree, 36 inches	12.60
19908	Folding Christmas Tree, 40 inches	16.20
19909	Folding Christmas Tree, 54 inches	42.00

FAVOR CHRISTMAS TREES

		GROSS
4011	Frosted Christmas Tree with Holly Berry, on Round Base, 3 inches...	$3.00
4012	Frosted Christmas Tree with Holly Berry, on Round Red Box, 3¾ in.	4.50
1940/55	Frosted Christmas Tree with Holly Berry, in Glass Pot, 3¾ inches......	4.80
11887	Frosted Christmas Tree in Red Wood Pot, 3 inches	4.80
19910	Frosted Tree in Red Wood Pot, 3½ inches	7.20
19911	Frosted Tree in Red Wood Pot, 4½ inches	10.80
19912	Frosted Tree in Red Wood Pot, 6 inches	12.00
19913	Frosted Tree in Red Wood Pot, 7 inches	15.00
5700	Christmas Tree on Green Wood Stand with Candles, 6½ inches	7.80
4013	Frosted Xmas Tree with Holly Berry, on Round Frosted Box, 5½ in.	9.25
4014	Frosted Xmas Tree with Holly Berry, on Round Frosted Box, 6½ in.	13.20

		DOZEN
19920	Christmas Tree with Red Holly Berries in China Pot, 6 inches	$3.60
214	Holly Plant Containing Snapper and Favor, 4 inches	.80
5702	Christmas Tree with Candles on Green Wood Stand, 9 inches	1.10
5703	Christmas Tree with Candles on Green Wood Stand, 13 inches	2.20

CHRISTMAS SEAL, TAG AND CARD CABINET

PER CABINET OF 50 ENVELOPES

40/604	Attractive Lithographed Display Cabinet Containing 50 Glazed Envelopes of Assorted Xmas Seals, Tags & Dinner Cards. Good value	$1.25

PER CARTON OF 50 PACKAGES

32/316	Christmas Seals, with Assorted Jolly Santas, 15 in Red Packet	$1.10
32/317	Christmas Seals, Round, with Santa and Poinsettia, 20 in Red Packet.	1.10
32/321	Christmas Seals, Large, Round, with Assorted Christmas Scenes, 6 in Red Packet.	1.10
32/320	Christmas Seals, Large, Round, with Comic Children, "Do Not Open Until Christmas," 6 in Red Packet.	1.10
32/322	Christmas Seals, Red Poinsettia, 15 in Red Packet.	1.10
32/325	Lithographed Christmas Card, with Assorted Pictures and Scenes, 8 in Red Packet.	1.10
32/327	Christmas Tags, with Red Strings, Assorted Pictures and Scenes, 6 in Red Packet.	1.10

All of the above items are neatly packed in red folding packets

CHRISTMAS NOVELTIES (Continued)
DRESSED KEWPIES FOR CHRISTMAS

		DOZEN
10/12	Celluloid Kewpie Santa with Painted Suit, Red Paper Cap and Beard Covered with Snow, 2½ inches........	$2.00
10/13	Celluloid Kewpie Wintersport Girls with Muffs and Muffler, Red Dress and White Cap Covered with Glistening Snow, 2½ inches.	2.00
10/113	Celluloid Kewpie Wintersport Boys, with Snowball and White Caps Covered with Glistening Snow, Red and White, 2½ inches.......	2.00
10/115	Celluloid Kewpie Toboggan Girl, Dressed in Red Dress and Red Turban Hat Trimmed with White Feathers, 2½ inches............	2.00
10/105	Celluloid Kewpie Holly Girl with Red Bonnet, Dress and Holly Tied in Hand, 2½ inches........	2.00
10/102	Celluloid Kewpie Christmas Girl with Large Red Hat and Plume, Holding Small Red Feathers, 2½ inches........	2.00

If so desired we can supply Dressed Dolls in all of the above styles at $1.50 per dozen.

10/12	80/115	55/104

		DOZEN
80/12	Celluloid Kewpie Santa with Painted Suit, Red Crepe Cap and White Beard Covered with Snow, 3½ inches........	$4.20
80/13	Celluloid Kewpie "Miss Snowtime" in Red and White Crepe Dress, with White Hat, Scarf and Muff Covered with Snow, 3½ inches.	4.20
80/144	Celluloid Kewpie "Holly Girl" with Red Dress and Bonnet Trimmed with Green Ribbon, Holding Holly in Mouth and Basket of Berries in Hand, 3½ inches........	4.20
80/107	Celluloid Kewpie "Tam O'Shanter" Girl with Red Dress and Bunch of Holly in Hand, 3½ inches........	4.20
80/115	Celluloid Kewpie Skating Girl with Red Dress and Turban Hat Trimmed with White Muffler and Feather, 3½ inches............	4.20
80/119	Celluloid Kewpie "Christmas Girl" with Red Fringed Dress and Hat, Holding Bunch of Holly, 3½ inches........	4.20

If so desired we can supply Dressed Dolls in all of the above styles at $2.25 dozen.

DRESSED CHRISTMAS CHINA KEWPIES

		DOZEN
55/104	China Kewpie Dressed in Bright Red Satin, Trimmed with White Fur and Attractive Trimmed Hat, 4¾ inches........	$9.60
55/117	China Kewpie Dressed in Attractive Red Crepe Dress and Up-to-Date Trimmed Hat with White Feather, Holding Bunch of Holly, 4¾ inches.	7.20
55/100	China Kewpie Santa Claus with Beard and Hat, Holding Tree, 4¾ inches	6.60
55/101	China Kewpie Snowman with Black High Hat and Snow Ball, 4¾	6.60
55/145	China Kewpie "Mildred," Artistically Dressed in Red Crepe and Pretty Maline Hat, Holding Bunch of Holly in Hand, 4¾	7.80
55/102	China Kewpie Christmas "American Beauty," Dressed Elaborately in Various Styles for Christmas in Silks and Maline, Trimmed with Holly and Gilt Ribbons, 5¾ inches........	10.20

CHRISTMAS NOVELTIES (Continued)
CHRISTMAS KEWPIES ON ROUND WHITE GLAZED BOXES

DOZEN

93/208   China Kewpie Doll, Dressed in Ermine Cape, Hat and Muff, Decorated with Poinsettia, mounted on frosted red crepe decorated 3 inch box.. $9.00

93/209   China Kewpie Doll, Dressed as Boy Skater with Sweater and Skating Cap, skates over shoulder, mounted on 3 inch box....................... 9.00

93/210   China Kewpie Doll, Dressed as Girl Skater, with Scarf and Skating Cap, mounted on frosted round box, 3 inches.............................. 9.00

93/211   China Kewpie Doll, Dressed as Santa Claus with Cotton Beard and Christmas Tree in arm, mounted on 3 inch round box.................. 9.00

LARGE DRESSED KEWPIES

Large China Kewpies, beautifully and artistically dressed in attractive costumes. Wonderful show window pieces.

103/7   China Christmas Girl Kewpie, Elaborately Dressed in Fluffy Maline Dress, Satin Bloomers Trimmed with Rosebuds, Large Attractive Satin Hat Trimmed with Holly and Ribbons, 9½ inches....   DOZEN $27.00

103/12   Kewpie, Dressed as Santa Claus, Carrying Bag Filled with Toys, Covered with Snow, 9½ inches... 24.00

103/13   Snow Man Kewpie, Covered with White Glistening Snow, and Black High Hat, 9½ inches.. 24.00

The above three numbers can be had in a 13-inch Kewpie Doll at an additional cost of about $12.00 per dozen.

HOLLY SPRAYS AND POINSETTIAS

32/352

32/219

GROSS

32/131	Holly Spray, 1 leaf, 1 berry, 2 inches..	$1.00
32/352	Holly Spray, 2 leaves, 2 berries, 3½ inches.................................	1.80
32/360	Holly Spray, 3 leaves, 3 berries, 4½ inches.................................	2.80
32/358	Holly Spray, 4 leaves, 4 berries, 5½ inches.................................	3.75
32/356	Holly Spray, 6 leaves, 6 berries, 7 inches...................................	7.80
32/359	Holly Spray, 9 leaves, 7 berries, 9 inches...................................	8.40
32/357	Holly Spray, 10 leaves, 7 berries, 9½ inches..............................	10.80
32/361	Mistletoe Spray, 9 leaves, 7 berries, 8 inches.............................	9.60
32/165	Red Velvet, Poinsettia with leaf, 3½ inches, on long stem...........	4.50
32/219	Red Velvet Poinsettia, with leaf, 7 inches, on long stem..............	8.40

DOZEN

31/300X	Red Celluloid Parasols, 2½ inches..	$ .70
31/301X	Red Celluloid Parasols, 3½ inches..	.85

35

CHRISTMAS NOVELTIES (Continued)
CHRISTMAS SNAPPING MOTTOES

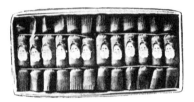

5543   94/84

Each motto contains a Snapper, Hat, Favor and Verse.

		GROSS
5543	Red Crepe Paper Motto with Santa Claus Picture, 12 mottoes to the box. Each motto 8 inches......................	$3.90
5539	Red Crepe Paper Motto with Fringed Ends and Santa Claus Head Picture. Packed 12 to the box. Each motto 6½ inches.............	4.80
5542	Red Crepe Paper Motto, with Fluted Ends and Large Santa Picture. Packed 12 to the box. Each motto 9½ inches...............	7.20
American Beauty	Red Crepe Paper Motto with Santa Claus Picture. Each motto 9 inches. 12 mottoes to the box......................	3.50
5550	Red Crepe Paper Motto, Spray of Holly on each motto, 6½ inches. 12 to the box......................	5.40
5552	Crepe Paper Motto, with Double Fringe Ends and Spray of Holly. Each motto 9 inches. 12 to the box. Can be had in red or white	8.40
144	Fringed End Crepe Paper Motto, with Holly Spray and Ribbon Bow. Each motto 8½ inches. 12 to the box. Can be had in red or white in attractive glazed boxes..........................	10.80
214	Red Flower Pot with Spray of Holly, Containing Snapper and Favor. 5 inches......................	9.60

THE "*ELSCO*" SNAPPING MOTTOES

DESIGNED and MANUFACTURED by us in our own FACTORY containing LARGE HATS, GOOD TOYS, MOTTO VERSE and SNAPPER. We use DENNISON'S BEST CREPE ONLY. Packed in strong WHITE GLAZED BOXES. A REAL AMERICAN PRODUCT. THEY ARE DIFFERENT.

		GROSS
94/75	Red Crepe Paper Motto with Crimped Ends and Frosted Holly Spray	$9.60
94/84	White Crepe Paper Motto with Crimped Ends and Frosted Holly Spray	9.60
94/79	Red Crepe Paper Motto with Crimped Ends Decorated with Poinsettia	9.60
94/210	Red and White Crepe Paper Mottoes with Crimped Ends Decorated with Holly and Poinsettia..........................	10.20
94/80	Red Crepe Paper Motto with Crimped Ends Decorated with Large Cotton Santa Holding Tree......................	11.40
94/82	Red Crepe Paper Motto with Red and White Crimped Ends Decorated with Frosted Holly Spray..........................	12.00
94/81	Red Crepe Paper Motto with Red and Green Crimped Ends Decorated with Frosted Holly Spray..........................	13.20

The above seven numbers are packed 12 to the box. Each motto 8 inches.

94/88	Large Rose Petal End Red Motto with Green Fringe Decorated with Double Frosted Holly Sprays and Berries, Red and Green Satin Ribbon Rosette, 6 to box, 13 inches	$14.40
94/86	Large Red Fringe End Motto, Red and Green Fringe Decorated with Large Holly Spray, 6 to box, 13 inches	13.20
94/85	Large White Motto, Red and Green Tulip Design Ends, Decorated with Large Holly Spray, 6 to box, 13 inches	13.20
94/87	Large White Motto with Snowball Design Ends, Decorated with Red Poinsettias and Green Fern, 6 to box, 13 inches	14.40
94/312	Large Red and White Motto with Tulip Petal Design Ends Decorated with White Frosted Snowballs and Holly, 6 to box, 13 inches	15.60

JUMBO CHRISTMAS "ELSCO" MOTTOES

DOZEN BOXES

94/102	Jumbo Christmas Motto, Red and Green Rose Petal Ends, Containing Large Noisemaker and Large Costume Hat, Decorated with Holly and Poinsettia Sprays, 3 to box, 18 inches	$13.20
94/102W	Jumbo Christmas Motto, White, with Red and Green Rose Petal Ends, Decorated with Pine Cones and Poinsettias, 3 to box, 18 inches	13.20

CHRISTMAS JACK HORNER PIES

92/222   92/224

THE "ELSCO" JACK HORNER PIES

Are CREATED by an EXPERT ARTIST and MANUFACTURED in our own FACTORY. Most ORIGINAL and DISTINCTIVE containing SPLENDID FAVORS for all occasions. DENNISON'S BEST CREPE only used.

92/241	Jack Horner Pie in Shape of Red Rose, Decorated with Holly Sprays, 9 inches high, 6 favors	EACH $1.50
92/227	Jack Horner Pie in shape of Tulip, Pointed Petal Design, Decorated with Snow and Poinsettias; 12 favors	2.25
92/224	Santa Claus with Toys on White Glistening Snowball Top, Decorated with Holly and Poinsettia, with 12 favors, 20 inches high	5.50
92/222	Russian Type Sled with Four Reindeers, Santa Driving, Back of Sled Filled with Toys, 12 favors, 30 inches long. Beautiful piece	12.50
92/221	Snow Man Pie, Large Snow Covered Figure with Red Clown Hat, and Pipe in Mouth Decorated with Holly and Poinsettia, 12 favors, 28 inches high	5.50
92/217	Large Glistening Snowball Pie, Decorated with Holly and Poinsettia, 12 favors, 14 inches tall	4.50
92/220	Large Glistening Snowball Pie, Decorated with Holly and Poinsettia, 12 favors, 18 inches high	4.50
92/238	Pine Branch Sled Pie, Nicely Decorated, Pulled by Four Reindeers with Santa Claus Driver on Base 9 x 24; 12 favors	8.50
92/240	Yule Log Pie, Attractively Decorated Yule Log Drawn by Two Large Reindeers with Santa Claus Mounted on Top on Base 12 x 27; 12 favors	10.00

SILVER TINSEL GARLANDS
A Most Effective and Attractive Decoration for the Tree and Room

Glass Ball   41/303   32/102

		GROSS YARDS
41/300	Silver Tinsel Garland, ⅜ inch thick, 6 yards on pc., 12 pcs. in box......	$1.20
41/301	Silver Tinsel Garland, ½ inch thick, 6 yards on pc., 6 pcs. in box........	1.80
41/302	Silver Tinsel Garland, ¾ inch thick, 6 yards on pc., 6 pcs. to box........	2.75
41/303	Silver Tinsel Garland, 1¼ inch thick, 6 yards on pc., 6 pcs. to box......	3.90
41/304	Silver Tinsel Garland, 1½ inch thick, 6 yards on pc., 2 pcs. to box......	5.75
41/305	Silver Tinsel Garland, 1¾ inch thick, 6 yards on pc., 2 pcs. to box......	7.80
41/307	Scalloped Silver Tinsel Garland, 1¾ inch thick, 6 yards on pc., 2 pcs. to box	7.80
41/322	Silver Tinsel Garland, 2 inches thick, 6 yards on pc., 2 pcs. to box........	10.20
41/323	Silver Tinsel Garland, 2⅛ inches thick, 6 yards on pc., 2 pcs. to box....	13.20

SILVER RIBBON ICICLES

GROSS BOXES

32/102	Silver Ribbon Icicles, a Realistic Reproduction of Silvery Shower, Made of Metal and Absolutely Fireproof. Packed in attractive lithographed box	$4.20

ANGEL HAIR AND TINSEL LAMETTA

GROSS BOXES

32/164	Soft Spun Glass Having Curly Hair Effect. Very attractive for the Tree	$9.00

GROSS ENVELOPES

32/370	Silver Lametta, Strands of Bright Silver Tinsel......	$2.75
32/369	Gold Lametta, Strands of Bright Gold Tinsel......	2.75

ARTIFICIAL CHRISTMAS SNOW

GROSS BOXES

32/103	Artificial Glistening Snow Flakes in Attractive Box Measuring 3x4¼ inches.	$4.20

TREE CANDLEHOLDERS AND FASTENERS

GROSS

32/189	Metal Christmas Tree Candleholder......	$1.10

GROSS BUNDLES

32/190	Twisted Wire for Fastening Ornament on the Christmas Tree...........	$ .90

GLASS ICICLES AND BALLS

DOZEN CARDS

9276/16	Glass Icicles, 12 on Card, 2½ inches......	$ .60
9276/18	Glass Icicles, 6 on Card, 4½ inches......	.85

We Have a Large Line of Imported Glass Balls, Glass String Balls, Fancy Glass Ornaments and Tree Tops. These We Make Up In Special $5.00, $10.00, $25.00 and 50.00 Assortments.

38

CHRISTMAS NOVELTIES (Continued)

41/313   13109   41/311

CHRISTMAS TINSEL ORNAMENTS

GROSS

41/317	Silver Tinsel Garland with Glass Ball, 8 inches............................	$1.50
41/313	Silver Tinsel Ornaments with Colored Glass Balls, 12 styles assorted in box, 4½ inches...	4.20
11831	Tinfoil Ornaments, Attractive Colored Tinfoil Ornaments in Shape of Flowers, assorted colors in box, 2½ inches........................	3.00
11838	Same style as above, but larger and prettier, 3½ inches....................	4.20

GLISTENING CHRISTMAS HOUSES, TREE ORNAMENTS

GROSS

13100	White Frosted Snow Houses, Beautifully Colored, assorted to box....	$12.60
13108	White Frosted Snow Houses, Beautifully Colored, assorted to box....	13.20
13109	Colored Frosted Snow Houses, Beautiful Assortment, 12 to box.........	13.80
13110	White Frosted Snow Houses, Beautifully Colored, 12 to box, larger sizes	16.20
13111	Colored Frosted Snow Houses, Beautiful Assortment, 12 to box, larger sizes	16.20
13107	White Frosted Fancy Shape Snow Houses, beautiful assortment, 12 to box	16.20

DOZEN

13106	White Frosted Silver Finish Snow Houses, Artistic Designs, Beautifully Colored, Assorted, 12 to box..	$1.95

CHRISTMAS CORNUCOPIAS AND HOLLY BOXES

GROSS

41/308	Cornucopia with Holly and Poinsettia Design with Red Crepe Paper Tops, 2 ounce container..	$1.50
41/309	Decorated Cornucopia with Tinsel Handle, ¼ lb. container...................	4.80
41/310	Cornucopia with Holly and Poinsettia Design, ¼ lb. container...........	3.25
41/311	Cornucopia with Holly and Poinsettia Design, ¾ lb. container.............	4.20
41/312	Cornucopia with Holly and Poinsettia Design, 1 lb. size........................	5.04

DOZEN

41/315	Holly and Poinsettia Boxes, Assorted Design, ½ lb. size......................	$ .60
41/316	Holly and Poinsettia Boxes, Assorted Designs, 1 lb. size.......................	.75

PER 100 SETS

41/314	Miniature Holly Box Set, 3 in set, oblong shape. Size ranging from 1¾ to 2½ inches. Suitable for coin or jewelry gifts...................	$6.50

FOLDING CHRISTMAS CANDY BOXES

34/337	Folding Christmas Candy Box with Holly and Poinsettia Decorations and Handle, ½-pound size...	GROSS $1.80

SILK RIBBON AND RIBBONZINE

PER SPOOL

Silk Baby Ribbon, all colors, 50 yards on spool..	$ .80
Silk Ribbon, all colors, ⅜ inch, 10 yards on piece....................................	.35
Ribbonzine, all colors, 500 yards on spool...	2.40

PER 100

Large Sheets of Printed Verses..	$2.25

CANDLES

PER 100 BOXES

Twisted Wax Christmas Candle, packed asst. colors, 48 to box...........	$10.00
Patent Wax Candles, Better Quality, 48 in box, packed solid colors....	19.00
Wax Tapers, Miniature Candles, 2 inches, 24 in box, packed solid color	3.00

CHRISTMAS NOVELTIES (Continued)
CHRISTMAS PAPER BELLS, GARLANDS, ETC.
PAPER BELLS

34/325   4010   34/330

		GROSS
34/321	Red Paper Folding Bell, 3 inches high	$ .90
34/322	Red Paper Folding Bell, 4 inches high	1.35
34/323	Red Paper Folding Bell, 6½ inches high	1.90
34/324	Red Paper Folding Bell, 9 inches high	4.00
34/325	Red and Green Paper Folding Bell, 9 inches high	4.00
34/327	Red Paper Folding Bell, 11 inches high	7.80
34/326	Red and Green Paper Folding Bell, 11 inches high	7.80
		DOZEN
34/328	Red Paper Folding Bell, 17 inches high	$1.75
34/329	Red and Green Paper Folding Bell, 17 inches high	1.75
34/330	Red and Green Paper Wreath, with Bell in center, 14 inches	.70

CHRISTMAS GARLANDS

		GROSS
34/332	Red and Green Folding Paper Garlands, 2¾ inches	$4.00
34/333	Red and Green Folding Paper Garlands, 3 inches	4.32
34/335	Red and Green Folding Paper Garlands, 4 inches	8.40
34/334	Red and Green Folding Paper Garlands, 6 inches	9.00
		DOZEN
34/337	Red and Green Folding Paper Garlands, 6x7 inches	$1.80
34/336	Red and Green Folding Paper Garlands, 9½ inches	2.00

FIBRE ROPE GARLANDS

		PER DOZEN BUNDLES
520/111	Red Fibre Rope Garland, 6 yards to bundle	$ .90

SANTA CLAUS BAG

		GROSS
4010	Red Net Christmas Bag, with Celluloid Santa Claus Head. Can be filled. 6 inches	$8.40

CHRISTMAS NAPKINS, CREPE PAPER FOLDS, ETC.

X290	Christmas Crepe Paper Table Covers, 63x84 inches	DOZEN $2.80
X926	Christmas Crepe Paper Napkins	PER 1,000 $3.00
X968	Christmas Folds Crepe Paper for Decorating	PER 100 $15.00

CHRISTMAS NOVELTIES (Continued)
CHRISTMAS FANCY PAPER CASES FOR SALTED NUTS

355/62   355/70   42/106

		GROSS
40/722	Oval Crepe Paper Basket with Rope Handle, Christmas Red and Green Combination.	$4.20
40/721	Square Crepe Paper Basket, with Rope Handle, Christmas Red and Green Combination.	4.20
40/700X	Oblong Crepe Paper Basket, with Rope Handle and Ribbon Bow	5.04
40/701X	Oval Crepe Paper Basket, with Rope Handle and Ribbon Bow	5.04
40/731	Oval Red Crepe Paper Basket, with Double Rope Handle	6.60

		PER 100
355/140	Round Red Fluted Crepe Paper Basket, with Double Rope Handle, Decorated with Santa Claus Cutout	$3.50
355/139	Round Red Fluted Crepe Paper Basket, with Double Rope Handle, Decorated with Holly Spray Cutout	3.50
355/69	Round Crepe Paper Covered Box, with Miniature Christmas Tree	7.75
355/61	Red Crepe Paper Basket with Santa on Handle	3.75
355/16	Red Crepe Paper Case.	3.00
355/59	Red Crepe Paper Open Case with Holly Spray	5.00
42/106	Red Crepe Paper Basket with Brass Bell on Handle	5.00
355/60	Red Crepe Paper Basket with Holly Spray on Handle	4.00
355/70	Red Crepe Paper Bell Box with Holly Spray	7.50

PAPER CASES FOR ICE CREAM

		PER 100
355/14X	Round Red Crepe Paper Basket with Rope Handle	$4.50
91/214	Red Crepe Paper Basket with Long Wire Handle and Velvet Poinsettia.	10.00
355/62	Round Red Crepe Paper Basket with Poinsettia on Handle	7.50
355/63	Round Red Crepe Paper Basket with Holly Spray on Handle	8.00
355/64	Round Red Crepe Paper Basket with Holly Spray and Santa	8.50
355/66	Round Red Crepe Paper Basket with Mistletoe Spray-on Handle	8.00
355/65	Round Red Crepe Paper Basket with Reindeer on Handle	12.00
355/58	Round Paper Box with Velvet Poinsettia	14.50
355/57	Red Satin Square Box with Holly Spray, 3½ inches	23.00
355/56	White Satin Square Box with Holly Spray, 3½ inches	23.00
32/167	Round Red Crepe Paper Box with Reindeer	24.00

		GROSS
40/724	Round Poinsettia Shaped Basket with Rope Handle	$6.60
91/213	Round Crepe Paper Ice Cream Case, with Holly Spray.	6.00
40/703	Red Crepe Paper Loving Cup, with Two Handles and Red Flower	12.00

		PER 100
93/272	Round Red Crepe Paper Covered Box, Decorated with Gold Bands and Small Christmas Tree on Top, 4 inches	$18.00
93/273	Same as 93/272 but size, 6 inches	25.00
93/274	Round Red Crepe Paper Covered Box, Decorated with Gold Bands and Small Reindeer on Top, 3½ inches	21.00
93/275	Same as 93/274 but size, 5 inches	30.00
93/276	Round Red Crepe Paper Covered Box with China Face, Brightly Dressed Top, Sitting on Top, Frosted Decorations, Very Attractive, 4x3 inches.	35.00
93/F.H.	Eskimo Snow House (Box) with Cute Snow Doll in Doorway, Frosted Decorations, Very Attractive, 4 inches	18.00

Our $25.00, $50.00 and $100.00 Christmas Assortments are given special attention and include the best selling and most attractive items.

NEW YEAR FAVORS AND NOVELTIES

72201A    12501   16702

		DOZEN
13452	Miniature Hour-Glass in Polished Wood Frame, 2¼ inches	$1.05
12501	Hour-Glass in Polished Wood Frame, 3½ inches	1.70
20/87	Celluloid Kewpie Doll Dressed as "Father Time," 2½ inches	1.50
32/96	Miniature Whiskey Bottle, "Gone But Not Forgotten," 2¼ inches	.30
32/97	Glass Whiskey Bottle, "Gone But Not Forgotten," 4 inches	.75
32/98	Large White Metal Badge, "Hootch Inspector," 2¼ inches	.35
8028	Miniature Cocktail Set of Four Pieces in 2-inch Box	.38
16729	Miniature Champagne Bottle (Box), 3¼ inches	.70
16702	Champagne Cooler, Bottle in Cracked Ice (Box), 3 inches	1.80
31/801	Prohibition Pump in Gilt Metal, 4½ inches	1.05
16711	Pressed Paper Camel, 3½ inches	.75
32/19	Miniature Rubber Boots "For the Wet Spots," in Box, 3 inches	3.60
11869	Cork, with Five Dice, 1½ inches	.60
16768	Silver Finish Cardboard Basket with Six Miniature Liquor Bottles, 3 inches.	1.85
1981/12	Cigar Butt with Five Bone Dice, 2½ inches	.60
1598	Miniature White Metal Cocktail Set. Four Glasses on Tray, 3 inches	1.35
6999/171	Wooden Beer Keg with Paper Snake, 2¼ inches	1.25
32/471	Miniature Metal "Brown Derby," 2 inches	.75

		DOZEN
14305	Champagne Bottle Snapper with Favor, 3 inches	.60
1010	Champagne Cork with China Sporting Girl's Head, 3 inches	6.00
100	Cork with Dancing Couple on Top, Fits in Wood Base, 5 inches	3.60
6999/169	Wooden Whiskey Bottle Containing Comic Snake, Assorted Colors, 4¼ inches.	1.00
9106	Large Cardboard Key, Silver Finish, "Key to Cellar," 7½ inches (Box)	1.90
2905	Miniature Wooden Champagne Set, Bottle with Four Glasses on Tray, Nicely Decorated, 1½ inches.	1.10
32/287	New Year's Book Containing Two Dice, 1½ inches	.70
12927	Miniature China Chamber Pot with Handle, 1¼ inches	.75
40/4048	Miniature China Steins, Assorted Mottoes, 1¼ inches	.25
72201A	Miniature White China Toilet with Lid "For Gentlemen Only," 2 inches.	1.00
1707	Miniature China Chamber with Handle and Gilt Lining, 1 inch	.70
1708	Miniature China Chamber with Handle and Gilt Lining and Comic Sayings, Can Be Used for Serving Drinks, 2 inches	1.50
417/3	Wooden Champagne Bottle Horn with Label, 5 inches	.70
21102	Miniature Cocktail Glass with Gilt Rim, 1½ inches	.45

MINIATURE LIQUOR BOTTLES

		DOZEN
12906	Miniature Cocktail Glass with Colored Liquid, 1½ inches	$.35
5947	Miniature Wine Decanter with Colored Liquid, 2 inches	.35
5545	Miniature Liquor Bottles, Assorted Shapes and Colors, 2 inches	.65
32/280	Liquor Glass Filled with Colored Liquid, 3 inches	.35
9516/15/1	Wine Glass Filled with Colored Liquid, 3½ inches	.55
9516/19/2	Large Wine Glass Filled with Colored Liquid, 4¼ inches	1.00
21100	Miniature Wine Bottles with Colored Liquid and Fancy Label, 2 inches.	.30

NEW YEAR FAVORS AND NOVELTIES (Continued)

32/79   32/185

GLASS CONTAINERS

		DOZEN
108	Imitation Cigar with Glass Filler and Cork. For Stag Parties, Banquets, Parties, etc., 5½ inches....................	$.50
32/36	Firecracker Box Marked "One Shot," Containing Glass Bottle, 3 inches.	1.10
32/79	Leatherbound Book Marked "Spring Poems"—The Four Swallows, Containing Four Glass Nip Bottles, Snuggly Fitted. When Pressed on Side at Thumb Mark, Top Opens, Disclosing Bottles, 3½x5½ inches.	21.00

NEW YEAR SOUVENIR NOVELTIES AND FIGURES

		DOZEN
561	Paper Man Dancing Figure, Nicely Colored, 9 inches................	$1.50
515	Paper Woman Dancing Figure, Nicely Colored, 9 inches..............	1.50
32/188B	Comic Woolen Dancing Figure on Base, Holding Whiskey Bottle, 5½ inches.	3.60
3999	Woolen Dancing Figures, Assorted Colors and Positions, 3 inches.......	2.00
12750	Nude Woman Figures, Assorted Positions, 2 inches..................	3.25
7009	Nude Woman Figures, on Base, Graceful Poses, 8½ inches............	19.80
205A	Satin Vanity Bag with Puff and Mirror, Assorted Colors, 3 inches......	2.25
32/13	Gilt Metal Vanity Box with Puff and Mirror, 1½ inches..........	1.50
32/242	White Metal Vanity Box with Powder, Puff and Mirror, 2½ inches....	2.40
32/283	Gilt Metal Vanity Box with Powder, Puff and Mirror, 2½ inches......	3.50
32/185	Assorted Color Glass Powder Vase with Kewpie Puff, 5 inches...........	16.20
32/465	Bone Cigarette Holder with Decorated Amber Tip, 4½ inches............	1.00
32/490	Bone Cigarette Holder with Decorated Amber Tip, Extra Long, 7 inches.	1.65
3509/8639	White Celluloid Folding Fan, 5½ inches..................	1.90
32/312	Decorated Metal Cigarette Case, 3½ inches................	4.00
32/64	Silver Metal Bud Vase, 4 inches................	4.20
60/1056	White Metal Memo Book with Pencil, 2½ inches..................	2.25
60/1057	Gilt Metal Memo Book with Pencil, 2½ inches..................	2.25
32/463	Leather Covered Memo Book with Loose Leaves, 3 inches...........	2.20
2100/2	Bone Cigarette Holder with Colored Glass Tip in Screw Top, Decorated Bone Case, 2½ inches................	4.80
2100/3	Bone Cigarette Holder with Colored Tip and Ash Tray to Match, 2 inches.	3.00
2100/4	Bone Cigarette Holder with Colored Decorated Tip and Ash Tray to Match, each set in handsome brocade box, 3¼ inches...........	5.40
32/11	Bone Shell Shape Dice Box with Five Small Dice, 2¼ inches...........	6.00

NOISEMAKERS

34/601

106

		GROSS
1981/6	Gold Tip Cigarette Horn, 3¼ inches	$1.50
1981/7	Colored Striped Cigarette Horn, 3¼ inches	1.50
1981/2	Colored Cigarette Holder Horn with Comic Face, 4 inches	2.40
1981/5	Cigar Horn, 4 inches.	3.00
8062	Red, White and Blue Metal Cricket, 2 inches	.90
8063	Decorated Metal Beetle Shape Cricket, 2 inches	.90
32/273	Rubber Nose Blower with Wooden Mouth Piece, 4 inches	4.80
32/57	Barking Dog Metal Head with Rubber Bulb, 3½ inches	9.60
32/182	Wooden Clapper with Handle and Two Spring Hammers, 5½ inches.	4.50
18716	Paper Pipe Horn with Wooden Mouthpiece, 6¼ inches	4.80
18714	Paper Trumpet with Wooden Mouthpiece, 3 inches	3.60
601/522	Decorated Wooden Whistle, 2¼ inches	3.60
32/191	Wooden Klitter Klatter Rattle, 6 inches	9.00
503/1	Painted Wooden Horn with Handle, 4 inches	4.80
106/1R	Painted Wooden Clapper with Two Hammers, 4 inches	4.80
30/302	Flat Carnival Clapper with Two Hammers, 6 inches	4.50
34/601	Wooden Thunder Rattle, 6 inches	10.20
34/600	Wooden Carnival Rattle with Two Clappers, 6 inches	4.20
34/602	Metal Frying Pan Rattle with Two Clappers, 8 inches	5.04
32/25	White Metal Rooter with Crank, 2½ inches	9.00
15872	Bright Metal Musical Horn with Handle, 3 inches	14.40
106	Mama Horn with Wooden Mouthpiece and Moving Tongue, 3½ inches.	4.20
1166/3	Square Decorated Wooden Double Hammer Clapper, 6 inches	4.00
1166/4	Round Decorated Wooden Double Hammer Clapper, 6 inches	4.00
32/456	Colored Wooden Box Shape Clapper, 8½ inches	7.50
32/445	Colored Wooden Clapper, 8½ inches	7.50

WHISTLES

		GROSS
6999/181	Bright Metal Whistle with Ring, 1½ inches	$1.50
6999/182	Bright Metal Whistle with Handle, 2¾ inches	2.00
6999/183	Bright Metal Pea Whistle, 1¾ inches	2.00
601/229	Gilt Metal Pig Whistle with Ring, 1½ inches	3.00
601/224	Gilt Metal Banjo Whistle with Ring, 2 inches	3.60
601/226	Gilt Metal Mandolin Whistle with Ring, 2 inches	3.60
601/231	Gilt Metal Pistol Whistle with Ring, 1¾ inches	3.60
601/228	Gilt Metal Whistle with Ring, 2½ inches	3.60
34/603	White Metal Whistle with Chain, 3½ inches	4.20
32/16	White Metal Siren Whistle, 2½ inches	10.20
15874	White Metal Double Musical Whistle with Ring, 6 inches	12.60
15884	White Metal Flute, 6 Keys, 9½ inches	8.40
32/15	Double Barrel, Silver Metal Whistle, with Ring, 4½ inches	9.00
34/604	White Metal Whistle, 2½ inches	4.50
8720	Wooden Pencil Whistle, 6 inches	4.80
8721	Colored Wooden Pencil Whistle, 6 inches	5.04
8722	Colored Wooden Pencil Whistle, 7 inches	8.40
1	Polished Natural Color Tree Stump Whistle, 6 inches	8.40
2	Polished Natural Color Tree Stump Whistle with Bird, 6 inches	12.00
32/473	Wooden Pipe Whistle Coming Comic Balloon Figure in Bowl, 3½ inches.	9.00

HARMONICAS

		GROSS
32/371	Miniature Watch Charm Harmonica, "Smallest in the World," 8 Notes, Splendidly Made, each in box	$14.40
32/241	Harmonica, each in box, 3½ inches	8.40

NOISEMAKERS (Continued)

32/34   35/301

CARDBOARD HORNS

		GROSS
17	Red, White and Blue Cardboard Horns, 6½ inches	$1.80
101	Red, White and Blue Cardboard Horns, 13½ inches	2.40
32/76	Red, White and Blue Cardboard Horns, 17 inches	3.00
35/302	Red, White and Blue Heavy Cardboard Horn, 7 inches	4.20
35/303	Red, White and Blue Heavy Cardboard Horn, 15 inches	9.25
35/301	Red, White and Blue Heavy Cardboard "Mama" Horn, 8 inches	9.25
111	Assorted Vegetable Horn, 9½ inches	16.20
8713	Red, White and Blue Paper Whistle, 2½ inches	3.00
		DOZEN
2700/1	Large Crepe Paper Covered Cardboard Horn with Assorted Crepe Paper Flower Ends and Streamers, 22 inches	$3.25

METAL COW BELLS

		GROSS
30/702	Heavy Copper Color Metal Cowbells, Small, 1 inch	$5.04
30/704	Heavy Copper Color Metal Cowbells, Medium, 1½ inches	7.20
30/703	Heavy Copper Color Metal Cowbells with Wrist Strap, 1-inch Bell	9.60
		DOZEN
32/496	Heavy Copper Color Metal Cowbell with Handle, 3¼ inches	$.85
30/700	Heavy Copper Color Metal Cowbells, 2¼ inches	1.45
32/492	Heavy Copper Color Metal Cowbells, 2¾ inches	1.95

METAL KAZOOS

		GROSS
32/33	Metal Kazoo, 4½ inches	$5.40
32/34	Metal Kazoo, Larger, Better Grade, 5 inches	7.20
75/44	Round Metal Kazoo, 2½ inches	5.40
		DOZEN
116	Gilded Trumpet Shape Kazoo, 12 inches	$1.50

METAL HORNS

		GROSS
15860	White Metal Horn with Handles, 3½ inches	$4.20
15861	White Metal Horns with Handle, 6 inches	9.00
15870	Decorated Metal Horn, Wooden Mouthpiece, 9 inches	8.40
15871	Decorated Metal Horn, Wooden Mouthpiece, 16 inches	13.20
15862	White Metal Trumpet with Handle and Tassel, 8 inches	10.20
		DOZEN
15883	Bright Metal Trumpets with Handle and Tassel, 12 inches	$1.65
15869	Bright Metal Trumpet with Handle and Tassel, 14 inches	3.25
		GROSS
36/403	Tin Horns, Assorted Colors, 6 inches	$4.20
36/400	Tin Horns, Assorted Colors, 12 inches	7.80
36/402	Tin Horns, Assorted Colors, 15 inches	12.00
		DOZEN
36/401	Tin Horns, Assorted Colors, 21 inches	$1.80
36/404	Tin Horns, Assorted Colors with Drum Shape Rattle End, 12 inches	.90

MUSICAL BELLS

		GROSS
6999/86	Silver Metal Bell with Black Wooden Handle, 2¼ inches	$4.50
6999/173	Silver Metal Bell with Black Wooden Handle, 3½ inches	8.40
6999/174	Brass Bell with Metal Handle, 2½ inches	16.20
6999/85	Musical Metal Bell with Long Wooden Handle, 6 inches	10.80
6999/81	Three Metal Bells on Wooden Handles, 7 inches	14.40
6999/84	Double Metal Musical Bell with Wooden Handles, 7 inches	19.20
6999/82	Nine Metal Bells on Wooden Handle, 8 inches	19.80

NOISEMAKERS (Continued)

| 32/61 | 8725 | 32/183 |

BALLOON NOISEMAKERS

GROSS

32/424	Balloon Horn with Wooden Blower, 5 inches	$4.20
32/62	Balloon Horn with Wooden Blower, 8 inches	8.40
32/61	Balloon Horn with Wooden Blower, Big Noisemaker, 12 inches	24.00
601/1112	Black and White Clown Head Balloons, with Whistle, 5 inches	9.60
32/183	Chinaman Head Balloon with Pigtail. When pressed, it makes a barking sound, 6 inches.	10.20
32/186	Black Cat Balloon on Legs with Wooden Squeaker, 6 inches	9.60
32/37	"Broadway Chicken" Balloon with Feather and Wooden Squeaker, 5 inches.	10.20
32/300	"Billy Goat" with Squeaker, 4 inches	9.60

DOZEN

| 32/458 | Comic Figure Balloon Squeaker "Noyzee Jim," Assorted Colors, with patent valve with Farm Yard noises in envelope, 6 inches. | $1.65 |
| 32/397 | Comic Figure Balloon with Painted Face and Patent Valve, 10 inches. | 2.00 |

BALLOONS

GROSS

32/48	Rubber Balloon with Patent Valve, Assorted Colors, Good Quality, 3 inches.	$3.60
32/60	Chinaman Head Balloon with Pigtail and Patent Valve, 3 inches	5.04
32/469	Miniature Round Balloon, Assorted Colors, 2½ inches	1.60
32/470	Miniature Sausage Shape Balloon, Assorted Colors, 3½ inches	1.60
32/479	Round Silver Balloon with Patent Valve, 3 inches	4.80
32/457	Football Shape Balloon, Assorted Colors, 4 inches	7.80
32/437	Large Round Balloon, Assorted Colors, 5 inches	9.60
32/474	Comic Clown Figure Balloon with Patent Valve, 6½ inches	9.60
32/475	Comic Fat Man Balloon on Legs with Patent Valve, 8 inches	15.00
32/301	Dumbell Balloon, Two Black Balloons with Cardboard Handle. When blown up represents a dumbell, 6 inches.	10.20

THE BALLOONS NUMBER 32/48 CAN BE HAD WITH SPECIAL
ADVERTISING
PRINTING AT AN ADDITIONAL COST OF ONE DOLLAR PER
GROSS IN LOTS OF FIVE GROSS OR MORE. ONE WEEK'S
TIME REQUIRED FOR SPECIAL PRINTING.

BLOWOUTS

GROSS

1166/6	Paper Blowouts, 15 inches	$1.80
1166/7	Paper Blowouts with Feather and Whistle, 22 inches	3.00
1166/8	Paper Blowouts with Feather and Whistle and Long Mouthpiece, 42 inches.	6.60
355/42	Crepe Paper Rose with Blowout, Assorted Colors, 11 inches	7.80

WOODEN RATCHET NOISEMAKERS

GROSS

18706	Wooden Ratchet Noisemaker, 3½ inches	$3.60
18707	Wooden Ratchet Noisemaker, 5 inches	4.80
677/3/2	Wooden Ratchet Noisemaker, 7 inches	9.00
32/31	Red, White and Blue Wooden Ratchet Noisemaker, 6 inches	5.40
32/32	Red, White and Blue Wooden Ratchet Noisemaker, 9 inches	9.60
512/9	Red Wooden Ratchet, 5 inches	8.40

NOISEMAKERS (Continued)

MUSICAL NOVELTY NOISEMAKERS

| 32/393 | 2094 | 32/374 |

		DOZEN
16020	Round Music Box with Handle, 3 inches	$.65
16021	Round Music Box with Handle, 4 inches	1.10
13738	Round Music Box with Handle, 5½ inches	3.25
156/1	Musical Chime Box with Handle, Nicely Decorated, 5½ inches	.40
15936	Musical Chime Box with Handle, Nicely Decorated, 7½ inches	.70
19501	Whiskey Bottle Shape Chime Box, 6 inches	1.50
19502	Musical Baby Nursing Bottle Chime Box, 7 inches	1.50
13702	Bright Metal Horn with Music Bell, 5 inches	.90
74/1	Cone Shape Bright Metal Horn, 4½ inches	.45
13715	Hunters' Knife with Bright Metal Mountings and Ribbon, 9½ inches	1.90
13704	Banjo Shape Music Box with Handle, 10½ inches	3.25

COMIC NOISEMAKERS

		GROSS
8729	Comic Wooden Figure Whistle, 3 inches	$9.00
8726	Wooden Champagne Bottle Horns, 4½ inches	9.00
2094	White Wooden Nursing Bottle Horns, 5½ inches	9.60
15925	Comic Baby Face Squeaker, 2 inches	4.20
12231	Comic Baby Face Squeaker, 2½ inches	8.40
35/300	Pocket "Cat Cry" Squeakers, 2¼ inches	9.00
8724	Wooden Horns with Horse's Head, 5 inches	5.40
8725	Wooden Horn with Donkey Head, 5 inches	8.40
8703	Comic Painted Bird Horn, 3½ inches	12.00
8710	Wooden Horn, Well Painted, 6½ inches	9.00
8717	Wooden Horn, Imitation Pacifier, Well Painted, 4 inches	8.40
8700	Comic Figure Wooden Horn, Well Painted, 5½ inches	12.00
8702	Wooden Cuckoo Bird, Well Painted, 4 inches	10.80
8728	Wooden Painted Devil Figure Horn, 6 inches	12.00
8709	Painted Wooden Horn with Double Rattle, 8½ inches	16.20
115/1	Wooden Enamel Mallet, 7 inches	8.40
15889	Metal Rattle with Whistle, 4 inches	5.04
32/374	Cardboard Buzzer Noisemaker with Handle, 12 inches	4.50
32/275	Painted Metal Tambourine, 6½ inches	10.20
		DOZEN
9863/11/20	Skin Covered Wooden Tambourine with Bells, 8 inches	$3.25
		DOZEN PAIRS
32/425	Bright Gilt Metal Cymbals, 5½ inches	$1.10
		DOZEN
9834	Barking Dog Squeaker, 4½ inches	$.95
1077/4	Double Bird Squeaker with Long Handle, 9 inches	1.00
8712	Wooden Whistling Bird Warbler with Handle, 8 inches	1.70
		GROSS
32/393	Metal Rattler with Painted Green Frog Design and Wooden Handle, 4 inches	$5.04
109	R. W. & B. Cardboard Horn with Comic Head and Tissue Streamer, 16 inches	8.40
11652	Cardboard Horn with Fringe Decorations, 18 inches	4.50
11651	Cardboard Horn with Fringe Decorations, 24 inches	8.40

CONFETTI AND SERPENTINES

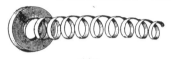

32/68   14656/2½

		PER 100
32/222	Glassine Paper Tubes Filled with Assorted Confetti, 5½ inches........	$3.00

		GROSS
10000/5	Tissue Paper Balls of Assorted Confetti, 2 inches...............................	$1.80

		DOZEN
704	Confetti Firecracker Bomb. When string is pulled, bomb explodes and showers confetti, 3½ inches...	$.75

		PER 1,000 ROLLS
32/68	Serpentine, Assorted Colors, 20 Streamers to Roll............................	$2.25

		GROSS PKGS.
520/183	Assorted Color Tissue Paper Streamers, 12 rolls to package................	$4.80
432/600	Assorted Color Tissue Paper Streamers, 18 rolls to package...............	8.40

		GROSS
14656/2½	Celluloid Balls Used as Confetti, 1 inch balls..	$1.80
14656/4½	Celluloid Balls Used as Confetti, 2 inch balls.......................................	4.80

NOVELTY INDOOR FIREWORKS

Fireworks for Banquets and all indoor parties. When lighted they burst showering contents of small Favors and cotton balls. A brisk all-year-round selling Party Novelty.

		DOZEN
700	Magic Orange, Containing Cotton Favors and Balls, 2 inches...........	$1.35
701	Magic Apple, Containing Cotton Favors and Balls, 2 inches...............	1.35
702	Magic Pumpkin, Containing Cotton Favors and Balls, 2 inches.........	1.35
706	Magic Candles, Containing Cotton Favors and Balls, 4 inches...........	1.35
705	Magic Flower Pots, Containing Favors, 2½ inches..............................	.70
14301	Magic Camera, Containing Cotton Favors and Balls, 2 inches...........	.85

		DOZEN BOXES
14318	Witch Serpent, 10 in box...	$3.60

SPARKLERS

		DOZEN BOXES
32/168	Sparklers, 10 in box, 8 inches...	.38
32/169	Sparklers, 5 in box, 14 inches............	.80

Magic Fruits

NEW YEAR NOVELTY DECORATIONS

		GROSS
32/376	Tissue Paper Shakers, with Stick, Assorted Colors, 28 inches...............	$4.20

		DOZEN
29	Paper Dressed Clown with Pierrot Figures on Long Stick, Assorted Colors, 28 inches.	$2.10
601/650	Pressed Paper French Cotillon Favors, Hammers, Knives and Hatchets, Tied with Large Bow and Kazoo in Bundle, 15 inches.	2.00
601/651	French Paper Flower Wands with Large Bow, Assorted Colors, 18 inches.	3.60
1207	Crepe Paper Flower with Favor, 8 inches..	.75
520/171	Decorated Paper Japanese Parasol, 24 inches...................................	2.75
214	Novelty Holly Spray in Red Flower Pot Motto, Containing Snapper and Favor, 4 inches.	.80
C.W.	Gilt Bamboo Wand with Chinese Figure, Well Made, Splendid for Cotillons, 60 inches.	7.20
520/209	Oil Paper Japanese Parasol, Sunproof and Waterproof, 36 inches..........	12.60

For **New Year Mottoes** see page 36.
For **Japanese Lanterns** see page 106.

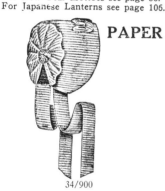
PAPER HATS

34/900	34/901

		GROSS
32/69	Pointed Crepe Paper Hat with Assorted Comic Figures.........................	$3.60
34/305	Scotch Paper Hat with Feather..	5.40
34/304	Decorated Paper Hat with Assorted Fairy Tale Pictures........................	4.80
34/303	Indian Hat with Paper Feathers..	4.80
34/302	Hussar's Hats with Red Pompom..	4.80
34/301	Pressed Paper Elk Hat.	5.40
32/253	Miniature Comic "Kiss Me" Hats to Fit Top of Head with Elastic......	3.60
R12577	Crepe Paper Hat with Long Plume...	4.80
32/378	Gold and Silver Crown Hats..	7.20
550	Black Crepe Paper Skull Cap..	6.60
95/119	Chinese Hat with Pigtail.	5.40
34/908	Black Paper Folding High Hat...	7.20
607	Comic French Duke's High Hat, Black Glazed Paper, with Elastic to Fit Top of Head..	9.60
32/279	Lithographed Red, White and Blue Hat with Paper Plume..................	4.80
34/900	Crepe Paper Sunbonnet with Paper Ribbons, Assorted Colors.............	13.20
34/901	Black and White Pointed Crepe Paper Hat with Clipped Paper Ends.	21.60
546	White Paper Chef's Hat.	6.60
11608	White Crepe Paper Turban Hats with Fringe...............................	4.80
12308	Checked Tissue Hat with Feathers...	4.20
11606	Chauffeur's Hat with Paper Goggles...	5.40
1000/292	Red Paper Hat with Long Tassel...	4.80
12312	Round Crimped Paper Hat.	3.00
100/291	Student's Hat with Tissue Tassels...	5.40
336	Tyrolean Hat with Feather.	5.40
40/713	Decorated Crepe Paper Hat with Tinsel Trimming.......................	9.60
11601	Round Paper Hat with Assorted Flowers..................................	7.20
364	Assorted Color Turban Hat with Paper Trimming.........................	6.00

PAPER HATS
(Continued)

34/301

32/69

		GROSS
202	Paper Hats, Assorted Animals	$6.00
201	Paper Hats, Tyrolean Design, with Feather	7.80
204	Crepe Paper Hat, with Comic Nodding Figure	5.40
203	Crepe Paper Hat, with Chicks and Roosters, Assorted	7.20
603	Chinese Hat, with Pigtails, Assorted Colors	9.00
11200	Jockey Cap, Assorted Colors	10.20
64	White Crepe Paper Sailor Hat	9.00
77	French Crepe Paper Sailor Hat, with Pom Pom	10.80
H24	Russian Soldier Hat, with Plume	8.40
35/805	Black Crepe Paper Skull Cap	6.60
		DOZEN
2733	Chinese Mandarin Hat, with Pigtail and Gold Trimmings	$1.65
8510	Black Pirate's Hat, with White Cut Paper Pom Pomps and Trimmings	1.65
8509	Crepe Paper Snake Charmer's Hat, with Snake Decoration, Assorted Colors	1.00
8504	Crepe Paper Hat, with Assorted Color Leaf Decorations	.85
8508	Crepe Paper Black Cat Hat	1.00
601/664	French Crepe Paper Hat, with Large Bow	.85
2090	Fancy Crepe Paper Hat, with Assorted Color Paper Plumes	1.20
2041	Ladies' Fancy Hat, with Assorted Ribbon Bow and Trimmings	1.20
8505	Black Crepe Paper Chinese Hat, with Pigtail and Orange Pom Pom and Tassel	.90
8503	Crepe Paper Fringed Hat, with Fancy Colored Band and Tassel, Assorted Colors	.85
8500	White Crepe Paper Hat Decorated with Assorted Color Flowers and Pom Poms	1.00
8507	Crepe Paper Old-fashioned Sunbonnet, with Ribbons, Pom Poms and Fringe, Assorted Colors	.75
8501	Crepe Paper Pointed Hat Decorated with Assorted Color Paper Leaves, Assorted Colors	1.00
8502	Crepe Paper Hat, with Paper Ribbons and Gold Trimmings	1.00
5711/3	Comic Red Derby Hat, with Artificial Hair and Nose	1.75
5711/1	Red Tissue Sailor Hat, with Rainbow Colored Streamers	1.05
118	Clown Hat, with Fringe Decoration and Pom Poms, Assorted Colors	1.00
5688/2	Bell Boy Hat, with Elastic Chin Strap, Assorted Colors	1.00
5711/7	Pointed Clown Hat, with Long Fringe Decorations	2.40
5711/5	Crepe Paper Turban, with White Feather and Fringe	3.40
5711/6	Sheik Hat, with Wide Gold Bands and White Feather	5.70
5711/4	Sheba Hat, with Gold Spangles and Long Veil	3.20

The above is a list of a few styles of Paper Hats we carry. Our line consists of two hundred different styles. We can make up assortments and will be pleased to submit samples for special occasions upon request.

MASKS

		GROSS
34/1	Black Linen Half Mask	$3.00
34/2	White Linen Half Mask	3.00
34/3	Assorted Color Linen Half Mask	3.00
34/11	Assorted Color Linen Mask with Curtain	4.50
34/4	Black Silk Half Mask	8.70
34/5	White Silk Half Mask	8.70
34/6	Assorted Color Silk Half Mask	8.70
34/7	Assorted Color Silk Mask with Curtain	19.20
		PER 100
34/9	Black and White Elastic with Fasteners for above Masks	$ .70

FAVORS

5201/5   49833    9092

Imported Pressed Cardboard Miniature Favors Cleverly Made and Can Be Filled

		DOZEN
9095	Miniature Dress Suit Case with Foreign Labels, 1½ inches	$ .38
9096	Miniature Dress Suit Case with Foreign Labels, 2 inches	.45
9097	Miniature Dress Suit Case with Foreign Labels, 2½ inches	.60
9101	Miniature Dress Suit Case with Foreign Labels, 3 inches	.80
9102	Miniature Dress Suit Case with Foreign Labels, 3¾ inches	1.10
9098	Satchel with Foreign Labels, 2½ inches	.75
9099	Satchel with Foreign Labels, 3¾ inches	1.00
9033	Round Hat Box with Handle and Foreign Labels, 1¾ inches	.60
9113	Round Hat Box with Handle and Foreign Labels, 2½ inches	.90
9018	Men's Hat Box with Handle and Foreign Labels, 1¾ inches	.75
49833	Men's Hat Box with Handle, Imitation Leather Finish, 1¾ inches	1.20
7760B	Large Attractively Colored Hat Box with Ribbon Bow, 3 inches	1.10
2370/76	Large Hat Box, Assorted Colors with Strap and Buckle, 3 inches	1.50
12394/997/1	Large Hat Box, Nicely Decorated with Strap and Buckle, 3¼ in.	1.50
9054	Hat Box, Assorted Colors with White Strap and Handle, 2½ inches	1.00
3511/8	Hat Box, Assorted Colors, with Foreign Labels and White Strap with Buckle, 4½ inches	3.00
5201/4	Floral Design Hat Box with Strap and Buckle, 2 inches	1.30
5201/5	Floral Design Hat Box with Strap and Buckle, 3 inches	1.80
5201/6	Floral Design Hat Box with Strap and Buckle, 4 inches	2.50
		PER 100
355/76	Shriner's Fez Hat Box, well made, 2½ inches	$8.50
		DOZEN
9028	Miniature Brown Curved Top Trunks with Foreign Labels, 1¾ inches	.70
9108	Miniature Glazed Curved Top Trunks with Foreign Labels, 1½ inches	.75
9017	Miniature Glazed Curved Top Trunks with Foreign Labels, 2 inches	1.00
9092	Curved Top Trunk with Foreign Labels, 3 inches	1.00
33/111	Brown Steamer Trunk, cheaper quality, 4 inches	1.00

The Above Five Numbers of Trunks Have Hinged Covers

		DOZEN
9094	Imitation Leather Suit Case, well made, 1¾ inches	$ .90
9093	Imitation Leather Suit Case with Tag, well made, 2¼ inches	1.30
49832	Imitation Leather Suit Case with Tag, well made, 3 inches	1.50
49861	Imitation Canvas Suit Case with Two Handles and Foreign Labels, 2½ inches	1.45
49852	Imitation Plaid Satchel with Straps, 3 inches	1.50
9024	Red Traveling Satchel, 2 inches	1.25
49838	Imitation Leather Flat Steamer Trunk, 2 inches	.80
9104	Imitation Leather Flat Steamer Trunk, 2¾ inches	1.05
9103	Imitation Leather Flat Steamer Trunk, 3½ inches	1.30
5201/1	Floral Design Dress Suit Case with Handle, 3¼ inches	1.00
5201/2	Floral Design Dress Suit Case with Handle, 3¾ inches	1.50
5201/3	Floral Design Dress Suit Case with Handle, 4½ inches	2.00
12394/458/1	Brown Imitation Leatherette Suit Case with Handle, 4 inches	1.60
9179	Tartan Color Miniature Emigrant's Suit Case with Straps and Handle, 3 inches	2.00

All Above Are Very Desirable and Brisk Selling Numbers for Bon Voyage Parties and All Other Occasions

FAVORS TO FILL (Continued)

	9064	9052	9060

Cat. No.	Description	DOZEN
706/310	Wooden Trunk Covered with Imitation Leather with Tray, Lock and Key, 4½ inches	$1.00
33/108	Imitation Tan Leather Suit Case, cheaper quality, ¼ lb. size	1.00
33/106	Red, White and Blue Suit Case, ¼ lb. size	1.00
9020	Imitation Wood Violin Case with Violin Inside, 3 inches	1.50
9064	Cigarette Case with Assorted Comic Pictures, which extend as box is opened, 3 inches	.42
9065	Same as No. 9064, but 4 inches	.70
9066	Same as No. 9064, but 5 inches	1.10
355/71	Miniature Straw Hat Box with Fancy Band, 4 inches	.65
9027	Miniature Red Music Bag with Handle, 1½ inches	.80
9019	Miniature Sled Box, 3 inches	.85
9029	Miniature Red Sled Box, 3 inches	.80
9062	Assorted Musical Instruments, sizes about 3 inches	.75
9105	Decorated Banjo, 3½ inches	.80
9026	Decorated Banjo, 4½ inches	1.00
9107	Decorated Music Roll with Straps, 4½ inches	1.30
9016	Black Camera with Handle, 2 inches	1.00
16702	Champagne Cooler with Bottle and Cracked Ice, 2¾ inches	1.80
16768	Silver Colored Wine Bottle Basket with 6 Bottles, 2½ inches	1.85
16730	Champagne Bottle, 3¼ inches	.65
9051	Imitation Mahogany Baby Grand Piano, 2 inches	2.00
9109	White Upright Piano with Floral Decorations, 3 inches	2.00
9050	Imitation Mahogany Upright Piano, 3 inches	2.00
9052	Imitation Mahogany Baby Grand Piano, 4 inches	3.30
9100	White Baby Grand Piano with Floral Decorations, 4 inches	3.60
3511/7	Miniature Floral Decorated Banjo and Mandolin Boxes, 4¾ inches	1.35
11864	Miniature Jewelry Bags and Trunks, assorted, 2½ inches	1.20
9060	Miniature Novelty Containers—Hats, Suit Cases, Bags, etc., 1½ in.	.85

	9020	 9050

Cat. No.	Description	DOZEN
3511/1	Novelty Cardboard Basket Box with Handle and Cover, Assorted Shapes and Colors, 2¼ inches	$1.00
3511/2	Book Shape Box, Decorated, Gilt Edge and Corners, 5¼ inches	3.20
3511/3	Nest of 6 Books, Combination of Colors, Decorated, 4 inches	3.60
3511/4	Imitation White Wood "Hope Chest" with Hinged Cover, 3½ inches	1.75
3511/5	Square Floral Decorated Box with Cover and Handle, 4¼ inches	3.20

FAVORS TO FILL (Continued)

33/124

33/131

Miniature Imitation Leather Suit Cases, Innovation Trunks, etc., Splendidly Made.
Natural Finish. Very Distinctive Novelty Candy Boxes.

		DOZEN
33/108	Imitation Leather Suit Case, ¼ pound size, 4 inches	$1.00
33/109	Imitation Leather Suit Case, ½ pound size, 5½ inches	1.35
33/124	Imitation Leather Kit Bag with Brass Locks and Handle, ¼ pound size, 4 inches.	2.25
33/125	Imitation Leather Kit Bag with Brass Locks and Handle, ½ pound size, 5 inches.	3.60
33/126	Imitation Leather Kit Bag with Brass Locks and Handle, 1 pound size, 5¾ inches.	7.20
33/130	Black Glazed Imitation Leatheroid, Curved Top Trunk with Brass Locks and Handles, 7¼ inches.	12.60
33/129	Black Glazed Imitation Leatheroid Ladies' Travelling Bag with Brass Locks and Handle, 9 inches.	18.60
33/131	Black Glazed Imitation Leatheroid Innovation Trunk with Drawers and Clothes Cabinet, Well Made with Brass Corners and Locks, size 9x5x5.	48.00
33/127	Black Glazed Imitation Leatheroid Hand Bag with Brass Locks and Handle, 5 inches.	14.40
33/133	Round Black Glazed Imitation Leatheroid Hand Bag with Brass Locks and Handle, 7¼ inches.	17.40

NOVELTY FANCY BOXES

		DOZEN
8006/0	Miniature Round Life Belt, Nicely Colored with Names of Steamships, 2 inches.	$1.20
8006/2	Miniature Round Life Belt, Nicely Colored with Names of Steamships, 3 inches.	2.10
2370/90	Imitation Wood Box of Cigars, Hinged Cover, 4¼ inches	3.60
2370/116	Miniature Set of School Books with Strap and Pencil, 4½ inches	3.30
2370/204	Miniature Book Cabinet with Books, 4½ inches	3.70
2370/121	Imitation Wood Roll Top Desk with Books and Blotter, 3¼ inches	3.40
3511/6	Square Gold and Silver Decorated Box with Cover and Handle, 4 in.	2.70
3511/9	Brown Imitation Leather Steamer Trunk with Foreign Labels and Hinged Cover, 3½ x 5½	3.00
3511/10	Novelty Kiddie School Book with Sliding Drawer and Bead Counting Frame Attractively Made, 5½ inches	5.25
3511/11	Horseshoe Shape Box Nicely Decorated with Colored Jockey Cap, 4½ inches	3.75

FAVORS TO FILL (Continued)

9030

9006

9090

OUTDOOR SPORT FAVORS

		DOZEN
9009	White Golf Ball, 1¾ inches	$.80
9006	Imitation Leather Golf Bag with Sticks, 4½ inches	1.50
9177	Imitation Plaid Golf Bag with Sticks, 5 inches	2.40
9178	Imitation Plaid Golf Bag with Sticks, 7 inches	3.50
7820/3	Imitation Plaid Golf Bag with Sticks, 8½ inches	4.65
9007	Tennis Racquet and Ball, 6½ inches	1.50
9008	Croquet Mallet, 4½ inches	.85
16749	Miniature Pair of Golf Clubs, 5 inches	1.00
9030	Imitation Baseball, 3¼ inches	.70
9003	Imitation Leather Football, 1¾ inches	.73
9004	Imitation Leather Football, 2¼ inches	1.10
9005	Imitation Leather Football, 3¼ inches	1.30
9086	Imitation Leather Football, 4¼ inches	2.25
9082	Imitation Leather Football, 6 inches	3.00
9083	Imitation Leather Football, 8 inches	4.80
15707	Imitation Leather Football, 2¼ inches, cheaper quality	.25
9023	Imitation Wood Bowling Ball, 2¼ inches	1.00
15708	Imitation Wood Bowling Ball, 2½ inches, cheaper quality	.38
9021	Imitation Wood Bowling Pin, 3 inches	.85
9022	Imitation Wood Bowling Pin, 4 inches	1.35
9010	Imitation Leather Basketball, 1½ inches	.80
152/1	Imitation Leather Basketball, 2 inches	1.25
9090	Imitation Leather Basketball, 2½ inches	1.60
152/3	Imitation Leather Basketball, 4 inches	2.90
152/4	Imitation Leather Basketball, 6½ inches	7.20
9016	Imitation Leather Kodak, 2 inches	1.00

9021

9007

IMITATION FRUIT AND NUT CONTAINERS

		GROSS
2377/1	Peanut, Open in Center, 2¾ inches	$3.60
2377/2	Peanut, Open in Center, 3¾ inches	4.80
2377/3	Walnut, Open in Center, 2¼ inches	4.80
15711	Red Apple, Open in Center, 2 inches	4.20
15709	Pear, Open in Center, 2¼ inches	4.20
15710	Lemon, Open in Center, 2 inches	4.20
2377/4	Potato, Open in Center, 2½ inches	4.20

FAVORS (Continued)

520/112

9069

355/32

FANCY BOXES ASSORTED SHAPES AND DESIGNS

		DOZEN
9069	Lithographed Boxes, Assorted Dutch Scenes and Children, 2½ inches.	$.45
9067	Lithographed Boxes, Assorted Dutch Scenes and Children, Telescope Cover, 2½ inches.	.70
9077	Lithographed Boxes, Children Assorted Comic Positions, 3½ inches.	.90
9076	Lithographed Boxes, Assorted Country Scenes, 3½ inches	.90
9070	Lithographed Boxes, Assorted Scenes from Grimm's Fairy Tales, Telescope Cover, 2¼ inches	.80
9071	Same as 9070, but 3½ inches	1.00
9072	Same as 9070, but 4½ inches	1.35
9073	Boxes Assorted Childhood Scenes, Telescope Covers, 4½ inches	1.35
9130	Lithographed Flower Design Boxes, Assorted Shapes and Colors, Telescope Covers, 2¼ inches	.65
9131	Same as 9130, size 3¾ inches	.75
9132	Lithographed Boxes, Children Pictures, Assorted Shapes, Telescope Cover, 3¾ inches.	.80
9124	Lithographed Boxes, Bird Designs, Assorted Shapes, 3½ inches	.80
9073	Lithographed Boxes, Assorted Children Comic Pictures, Assorted Shapes, 4¾ inches.	1.35
9127	Lithographed Boxes, Assorted Children Comic Pictures, Assorted Shapes, 4¼ inches.	.80
9125	Lithographed Boxes, Assorted Bird Design Pictures, Assorted Shapes, 4¼ inches.	1.05

RED, WHITE AND BLUE SHIELD AND DRUM BOXES

		GROSS
520/112	Satin Red, White and Blue Shield Box, 2¼ inches	$5.04
520/113	Satin Red, White and Blue Shield Box, 3 inches	8.40
520/114	Satin Red, White and Blue Shield Box, 3¾ inches	12.60
11861	Miniature Drum Box, 1½ inches	3.60
32/451	Miniature Red, White and Blue Drum Box, 2½ inches	4.50
11863	Miniature Red, White and Blue Drum Box, 3 inches	7.20
355/32	Miniature Red, White and Blue Drum Box, Better Quality, 1¾ inches.	7.20

		DOZEN
355/31	Red, White and Blue Uncle Sam Hat, 2 inches	$.78
33/114	Red, White and Blue Box with Toy Cannon Mounted on Top, 4 inches	.90
33/106	Red, White and Blue Suit Case, ¼ pound size	1.00

EGYPTIAN FAVORS (To Fill)

		DOZEN
16773	Egyptian Sphinx, Natural Color, 4 inches	$1.20
16775	Egyptian Pyramid, Natural Color, 4 inches	1.20
16776	Egyptian Obelisk, Natural Color, 5 inches	1.00
16774	Egyptian Mummy Figure, 4 inches	1.10

FAVORS (Continued)
HEART BOXES

520/116   9047    9043

9134	Curved Red Glazed Heart Box, with Cupid Picture, 2¾ inches............	$1.10
9135	Curved Red Glazed Heart Box, with Cupid Picture, 3¼ inches............	1.50
9013	Curved Red Glazed Heart Box, with Cupid Picture, 3½ inches............	1.80
9014	Curved Red Glazed Heart Box with Cupid Picture, 6 inches............	2.65
9047	Heart with Crepe Paper Bag with Forget-Me-Not Design, 2 inches.....	.60

GROSS

15704	Red Pressed Paper Heart Box, 1½ inches...................................	$3.60
15705	Red Pressed Paper Heart Box, 3 inches...................................	4.80
2118	Red Glazed Paper Heart Box, 1¾ inches...................................	5.04
2119	Red Glazed Paper Heart Box, 2½ inches...................................	7.80
2120	Red Glazed Paper Heart Box, 3½ inches...................................	11.40

DOZEN

2121	Red Glazed Paper Heart Box, 4½ inches...................................	$1.35
2122	Red Glazed Paper Heart Box, 5 inches...................................	2.70
9002	Red Glazed Blocked Heart Box, 1½ inches...................................	.70

DECORATED HEART BOXES
DOZEN

9012	Heart Box Decorated with Forget-Me-Nots, 1½ inches........................	$.65
9063	Heart Box with Lithographed Cupid Picture, 1½ inches........................	.90
9042	Flat Red Cardboard Heart Box with Cupid Picture, 2¼ inches............	.65
9043	Flat Red Cardboard Heart Box with Cupid Picture, 3 inches............	.85
9044	Flat Red Cardboard Heart Box with Cupid Picture, 4½ inches............	1.20
9045	Flat Red Cardboard Heart Box with Cupid Picture, 5¾ inches............	1.80

RED SATIN HEART BOXES
GROSS

520/116	Red Satin Heart Box with Padded Top, 2¼ inches................................	$4.50
520/117	Red Satin Heart Box with Padded Top, 3 inches................................	8.40
520/118	Red Satin Heart Box with Padded Top, 3¾ inches................................	11.40

RED SATIN HEART BOXES
Heavy Quality, Well Made
PER 100

355/110	Red Satin Heart Box, 2¼ inches..	$6.25
355/111	Red Satin Heart Box, 2¾ inches..	7.50
355/112	Red Satin Heart Box, 3½ inches..	9.50
355/113	Red Satin Heart Box, ¼ pound size..	18.50

DOZEN

355/114	Red Satin Heart Box, ½ pound size..	$3.10
355/115	Red Satin Heart Box, 1 pound size..	4.25
355/116	Red Satin Heart Box, 2 pound size..	6.40
355/117	Red Satin Heart Box, 3 pound size..	10.20
9056	Red Satin Blocked Heart Box with Padded Top, 2¼ inches..................	2.20
9057	Red Satin Blocked Heart Box with Padded Top, 3 inches..................	3.20
5102/5	Red Satin Heart Box with Padded Top, Single Layer, ½ pound size...	4.50
5102/6	Red Satin Heart Box with Padded Top, Single Layer, 1 pound size.....	6.75
5102/7	Red Satin Heart Box with Padded Top, Single Layer, 2 pound size.....	9.80

FAVORS (Continued)
MISCELLANEOUS NOVELTY BOXES

355/24   33/100

		DOZEN
9053	Imitation Wood Billiard Tables, 2¾ inches..	$2.00
355/76	Red Fez Hat with Silk Tassel, 2½ inches..	1.00
7503	Lithographed Cutouts with Box, Assorted Fairy Tales, 3 inches...........	.75
9000	Miniature Globe, 1½ inches..	.90
9001	Miniature Globe on Wooden Stand, 3½ inches	1.35
9110	Miniature Rattle with Wooden Handle, 3½ inches; can be filled.........	.85
11864	Miniature Favors, 12 Assorted Styles in Box; Trunks, Bags, etc.; about 2½ inches.	1.20
49837	Miniature Dog Carrier with Little Dog, 1¾ inches..................................	1.70
16020	Decorated Music Box with Handle, 2 inches..	.65
6999/165	Decorated Music Box, with Handle, 2½ inches..	1.00
6999/166	Decorated Music Box, with Handle, 2¾ inches..	1.20
11867	Church with Steeple, 4 inches..	.70
20600	Miniature Country Houses, Assorted, 2 inches..	.35
20602	Decorated Country Houses, Assorted, 4 inches..	1.70
355/24	Card Table with Cards on Top, 3 inches..	1.20
33/100	Wall Telephone, 5 inches..	1.20
355/122	Miniature Dice Box, 1½ inches..	.72
161/2a	Miniature Market Basket with Lid and Handle, Attractively Colored, 2¼ inches.	.70

COMPOSITION FOOTBALLS

		GROSS
725/100	Composition Football on Pin, 2 inches..	$4.50
725/99	Composition Football, Natural Color (Box), 2¼ inches..........................	7.20
725/101	Composition Football, Natural Color (Box), 3¼ inches..........................	13.20
		DOZEN
725/102	Composition Football, Natural Color (Box), 4¾ inches..........................	3.00
725/103	Composition Football, Natural Color (Box), 5¾ inches..........................	6.25
		DOZEN
16777	Egyptian Warrior Mounted on Camel, Nicely Colored and Well Made, 4 inches.	$2.70
16778	Polo Player on Horseback, Nicely Colored, 4½ inches..........................	2.10
16779	Parrot on Swing, Well Made and Nicely Colored, 8 inches....................	2.20
16781/1	Assorted Palette, Well Made, 2¼ inches..	.55

PRESSED PAPER NOVELTIES

Exceptionally Well Made and Can Be Used for Hanging and Decorating

	16749	16742	16715

		DOZEN
16712	Miniature Camel, 2 inches	$.38
2417/11	Silver and Gold Fish, 3 inches	.38
2417/44	Silver and Gold Reindeer, 2½ inches	.40
2417/28	Silver and Gold Walnut, 2 inches	.35
16743	Red Lobster, 2 inches	.35
2417/50	Red Lobster, 4 inches	.55
2417/30	Red Heart, 2 inches	.40
2417/31	Silver and Gold Revolver, 4 inches	.55
16732	Glazed Red Heart, 1 inch	.25
16734	Silver Glazed Heart, 1 inch	.25
16733	Gold Glazed Heart, 1 inch	.25
16708	Brown Fox, 4 inches	.75
16713	Brown Moose, 2 inches	.38
16703	Brown Reindeer, 2 inches	.38
2417/35	White Rooster, 3 inches	.38
16701	Brown Reindeer, 3½ inches	.70
16705	Brown Moose, 3½ inches	1.00
16706	Natural Color Lion, Glass Eyes, 4½ inches	1.00
16717	Eagle with Spread Wings, Glass Eyes, 6 inches	1.00
16709	Brown Bison, 4 inches	1.00
16707	White Polar Bear, 4 inches	.80
16711	Brown Camel, 3 inches	.60
16716	Black and White Billy Goat, 4 inches	.75
16704	Natural Color Pig, 3½ inches	.80
16715	Grey Elephant, 4½ inches	1.35
16710	Brown Horse, 4 inches	.75
16720	White Stork, Well Made, 3½ inches	1.00
16740	Pair Silver Skates, 2 inches	1.00
16742	Sail Boat, Gilded Keel, 3 inches	.90
16747	Brown Owl, Glass Eyes, 3 inches	1.00
16749	Miniature Pair Golf Clubs, 5 inches	1.00
16750	Slippers with Open Bag, 3 inches	.65
16748	Miniature Roast Turkey, 2 inches	.55
16751	Silver Violin with Bow, 3½ inches	1.20
16748/1	Silver Horse Shoe, 1¼ inches	.25
16738	Cupid with Wings, 1½ inches	.55
16752	Silver Slipper with Silk Bag, 3 inches	.85
16753	Silver Slipper with Silk Bag, 4 inches	1.20
16731	Foreign Court Orders with Silk Ribbon, Exact Imitations, 12 Assorted in Box.	.75

		GROSS
16745	Green Frog, 2 inches	$7.80
1007/56	White Rabbit, 3 inches	4.80
16746	White Fishing Net, 3½ inches	3.00
16744	Green Frog on Ladder, 2 inches	3.00
16760	Pressed Paper White Dove, 2½ inches	5.04
16761	Pressed Paper White Duck, 3 inches	9.00

METAL NOVELTIES

ATTRACTIVE LINE OF MINIATURE FAVORS AND DOLL HOUSE NOVELTIES

1187/106	1187/60	1187/75

		DOZEN
1187/106	Miniature Chafing Dish, 3 Separate Sections, 2 inches	$2.00
1187/25	Miniature Phonograph with Horn and Handle, 2½ inches	2.40
1187/68	Miniature Clothes Wringer, Rubber Rollers, 2½ inches	2.50
1187/19	Miniature Radiator, 2½ inches	2.50
1187/60	Miniature Carpet Sweeper, 6 inches	1.80
1187/42	Miniature Sewing Machine, 3 inches	2.90
1187/104	Miniature Sewing Basket on Stand, 3 inches	2.20
1187/98	Miniature Sewing Basket with Thimble and Scissors, 2½ inches	2.20
1187/83	Miniature Baby Carriage with Cloth Hood, Pink and Blue, 2½ inches.	2.20
1187/109	Miniature Gilt Metal Doll Dresser with Mirror, Brush and Comb, 4 inches.	2.75
1187/84	Miniature Go-Cart, 2½ inches	1.85
1187/3	Miniature Baby Crib with Doll, Canopy and Draperies, 3 inches	2.50
1187/17	Miniature Ironing Set with Iron, Basket, Board and Dish, each set in box, 5x2½ inches.	2.70
1187/24	Miniature Gas Stove with Rubber Pipe, Frying Pan and Pot, 3 inches.	3.40
1187/103	Miniature Percolator with Cover and Heater, 1½ inches	1.35
1187/29	Miniature Fireplace, with Imitation Fire, 2½ inches	3.25
1187/57	Miniature Gilt Metal Tea Table with Wheels and Small Plates of Eatables, 2¼ inches.	3.25
1187/66	Gilt Metal Bird Cage, 2 inches	.90
1187/72	Gilt Metal Clock with Mirror, 2½ inches	3.25
1187/70	Gilt Metal Parlor Lamp, 2½ inches	2.70
1187/73	Gilt Metal Fruit Tray with Handle, Containing Fruit and Knife	1.35
1187/75	Vinegar and Oil Bottles on Metal Caster Stand, 2 inches	1.65
1187/79	Clothes Wringer with Rubber Rollers, 2½ inches	3.25
1187/80	Writing Set, Two Glass Ink Wells and Pen on Metal Stand, 2½ inches	2.50
1187/82	Miniature Brown Thermos Bottle, 1½ inches	1.75
1187/110	Vacuum Cleaner with Tank and Rubber Hose, 1½ inches	1.90
1187/111	Gilt Metal Medicine Chest, Containing Tiny Bottles and Roll of Bandage, 2 inches.	3.20
1187/112	Smokers' Set on Metal Tray, 2½ inches	1.80
1187/113	Gilt Bird Cage on Stand Decorated with Flower Pots on Both Sides, 4½ inches.	2.25
1187/114	Glass and Metal Cheese Dish with Knife, Containing Cheese, 1¾ inches	1.50
1187/116	Miniature Toast Rack, Containing Pieces of Toast, 1½ inches	1.70
1187/118	Miniature Fishing Rod with Line and Fish, 4 inches	.80
1187/102	Gas Range with Door, 2¾ inches	3.25
1187/88	Garden Set, Consisting of Hoe, Rake and Shovel on Card, 3½ inches..	.90
1187/115	Garden Set, Consisting of Hoe, Rake, Shovel and Sprinkling Can in 4-Inch Box.	1.95
1187/131	Miniature Glass Butter Dish with Engraved Cover, 1½ inches	1.45
1187/86	Miniature Gilt Swinging Cradle with Stand and Lace Canopy, 3 inches	1.70
1187/58	Miniature White Metal Telephone with Receiver and Movable Mouthpiece.	1.90
1187/77	Miniature Old Fashioned Telephone with Movable Receiver and Handle, 1 inch.	1.95
1187/56	Miniature White Metal Percolator with Heater, 2 inches	2.10
16001	Miniature Gilt Metal Radiator on Feet with Valve, 2 inches	1.50
1187/101	Miniature Metal Christmas Tree, Nicely Colored, 3 inches	1.80
2086	Miniature White Metal Cigar Stand with Cigars and Ash Tray, 3¼ inches.	2.25

METAL NOVELTIES (Continued)

1187/83    1187/113    6999/14   1187/112

MINIATURE ELECTRICAL DOLL HOUSE NOVELTIES AND FAVORS

		DOZEN
1187/135	Miniature Bronze Metal Samovar on Stand with Electrical Attachment, 2 inches.	$2.10
1187/136	Miniature Preserve Kettle on Stand with Electrical Attachment, 1½ inches.	2.00
1187/137	Miniature Chafing Dish with Electrical Attachment, 1½ inches	2.40
1187/138	Miniature Coffee Percolator with Electrical Attachment, 2¼ inches	3.25
1187/139	Miniature Baby Bottle Heater with Bottle and Electrical Attachment, 2½ inches.	2.40
1187/200	Miniature Imitation Electric Fan, 2½ inches	1.50
1187/201	Miniature Electric Heater, Electric Fan Shape	1.50
1187/140	Miniature Electric Toaster with Attachment	1.70
1187/145	Miniature Radio Set with Bulb and Head Piece, 2 inches	3.60
1187/146	Miniature Oil Stove with Handle, 3 inches	2.40

METAL DOLL HOUSE NOVELTIES AND FAVORS

		DOZEN
8056	Miniature Gilt Metal Writing Desk with Drop Front, 2¼ inches	$.85
8050	Miniature Gilt Metal Victrola with Lid that Raises, 2½ inches	.85
8052	Miniature Metal Tea Cart, Assorted Colors, 2 inches	.85
8053	Miniature Metal Standing Gas Range, 3 inches	.85
16000	Miniature Metal Parlor Stove, 3 inches	1.50
15942	Miniature Metal Umbrella Stand, Assorted Colors, with Cane and Umbrella, 2 inches.	1.00
6999/14	Miniature Metal Table Oil Lamp with Crystal Globe, 2½ inches	.80
15954	Miniature White Metal Gravy Boat, 1¼ inches	.50
16003	Miniature Gilt Metal Fruit Stand with Assorted Colored Glass Dish, 1½ inches.	.75
15948	Miniature Gilt Metal Table Lamp with Glass Shade, 2 inches	.90
601/40	Miniature Metal Billiard Table with Cues and Balls, 2½ inches	.40
6999/10	Miniature Gilt Metal Smoking Stand, 3½ inches	.80
7558	White Metal Basket with Cover, 2 inches	.85
7554	White Metal Parlor Stove, 3½ inches	2.10
35/600	White Metal Baby Carriage with Metal Hood and Movable Wheels, Each in Box, 3¼ inches.	1.75
35/608	Metal Piano, 4 inches	2.40
35/607	Metal Fireplace, 4 inches	2.40
6999/9	Miniature Carving Set on Wall Rack, 3¼ inches	.75
8005	Miniature Metal Desk Telephone, 3 inches	.40
8404	Miniature Mantel Clock with Movable Hands, 1 inch	.70
1408	Miniature White Metal Coffee Set, Complete with Tray, Each Set in Box, 2 inches.	1.35
2048	Miniature White Metal Coffee Set with Oblong Decorated Tray, Each Set in Box, 2¼ inches.	1.60
1097/3	Miniature White Metal Tea Set with Round Tray, Each Set in Box, 2¾ inches.	1.90
1097/2	Miniature White Metal Tea Set with Round Tray, Each Set in Box, 3½ inches.	2.25
1999	Miniature Picnic Case Complete with White Metal Tea Set, 3 inches.	1.90

METAL NOVELTIES (Continued)

15059    15032    15016   2006

WHITE ENAMEL DOLL HOUSE KITCHEN NOVELTIES AND FAVORS

15036	Miniature White Enamel Salt Box with Hinged Cover, 2 inches	$.70
15035	Miniature White Enamel Flour Box with Hinged Cover, 2 inches	.70
15031	Miniature White Enamel Sugar Box with Hinged Cover, 1¾ inches	.60
15032	Miniature White Enamel Coffee Grinder, 2½ inches	1.20
15033	Same as 15032, but 3½ inches	1.35
15038	Miniature White Enamel Pail, 2¾ inches	.75
15037	Same as 15038, but 4 inches	.80
15059	Miniature White Enamel Bread and Cake Box, with Hinged Cover, 2½ inches	1.90
6095/607/1	Miniature Blue and White Enamel Baby's Bath Tub, 3 inches	.70
15029	Miniature Enamel Trays, Assorted Colors and Designs, 4 inches	.70
6999/121	Miniature White Enamel Cook Set, Table, Gas Stove and Pots and Pans, each set on card, 5 inches	3.60
6890/3/1	Miniature White Enamel Baby Carriage, 5 inches	1.75
6999/8	Miniature White Enamel Coffee Grinder with Glass Receiver, 3¼ in.	1.05

		DOZEN
644/1	Miniature White Enamel Candlestick, 2¾ inches	$.85
677/1	Miniature White Enamel Kitchen Set, Three Brushes on Hanger, 5 inches	2.20
6850/32	Miniature White Enamel Cash Register with Keys, and Drawer that Opens When Handle is Turned. Splendidly Made, 3 in	6.25
13703	White Enamel Doll Crib, 3½ inches	.60
6095/137/3	Miniature Tin Dish Pan, 3 inches	$.42
6095/108/1	Miniature Tin Coffee Percolator, Two Pieces, 3½ inches	.80
6095/124/1	Miniature Tin Tea Pot, 3 inches	.75
6095/114/0	Miniature Tin Dust Pan, 4 inches	.30
6095/121/1	Miniature Tin Flour Scoop, 2¾ inches	.65
15015	Miniature Tin Grater, 3 inches	.35
601/111	Miniature Tin Colored Shopping Basket, Hinged Covers and Handle, 3 inches	.90
6999/7	Miniature Tin Wall Oil Lamp, 3 inches	.75

BRASS DOLL HOUSE NOVELTIES

		DOZEN
6095/407/1	Brass Cooking Pot with Long Handle, Well Made, 3½ inches	$.80
6095/407/3	Brass Cooking Pot with Long Handle, Well Made, 4½ inches	1.00
6095/407/4½	Brass Cooking Pot with Long Handle, Well Made, 6¼ inches	1.50
6095/408//1	Brass Dish Pan with Two Handles, Well Made, 2¼ inches	.75
6095/408/2	Same as 6095/408/1, but size 2½ inches	.85
6095/408/3	Same as 6095/408/1, but size 3 inches	1.00
6095/408/4	Same as 6095/408/1, but size 3¼ inches	1.50
15025	Same as 6095/408/1, but size 4¼ inches	2.00
6095/418/1	Brass Preserving Pan with Two Handles, 3 inches	1.50
6095/418/2	Same as 6095/418/1, but size 3½ inches	2.25
15028	Same as 6095/418/1, but size 4 inches	2.40
32/226	Brass Tripod Kettle with Handle, 2½ inches	.75
32/225	Brass Bucket with Handle, 2½ inches	.80
15016	Brass Candlestick with Handle, 3 inches	1.45
2006	Miniature Brass Coal Hod and Shovel, Well Made, 3 inches	2.00

METAL FAVOR MEMO BOOKS

8002	60/1056	8005	6999W/6

		DOZEN
32/252	White Metal Memo Book with Pencil and Pad, 2¼ inches	$1.35
601/900	White Metal Embossed Memo Book with Pencil and Pad, 2 inches..	2.10
601/901	White Metal Embossed Memo Book with Pencil and Pad, 3 inches..	3.60
601/902	Gold Metal Embossed Memo Book with Pencil and Pad, 2 inches..	4.00
601/912	Silver Metal Embossed Memo Book with Metal Pencil and Pad, 4 inches.	12.60
60/1056	White Metal Memo Book with Pencil and Pad, 2½ inches	2.10
60/1057	Gilt Metal Memo Book with Pencil and Pad, 2½ inches	2.10

MISCELLANEOUS METAL NOVELTIES AND FAVORS

15806	Metal Knife, Fork and Spoon Set with Napkin, Each Set in Box, 3 inches.	DOZEN $.50
15807	Metal Knife, Fork and Spoon Set with Napkin, Each Set in Box, 4 inches.	1.00
15808	Metal Knife, Fork and Two Spoons Set with Napkin, Each Set on Card, 4 inches.	.40
15809	Metal Knife, Fork and Two Spoons Set on Card, 4 inches	.35
15816	Metal Knife and Fork Sets with Black Wood Handle	.42
6095/3/3	Metal Knife and Fork Set with Red Handle, 4 inches	.85
12929	Metal Knife and Fork Sets with Bone Handle, 2 inches	.75
6095/3/1	Metal Knife and Fork Sets with Metal Handles, 2½ inches	.42
6095/181/1	White Metal Spoons, 3¼ inches	.30
6099/120	Metal Cooking Set, Stove, Pot and Pan, Each Set in Box, 3¾ inches.	1.00
8004	Painted Metal Horse on Stand with Wheels, 2 inches	.40
8001	Miniature Limousine, Assorted Colors, 1¾ inches	.40
8002	Miniature Metal Touring Car with Disc Wheels, Assorted Colors, 3 inches.	.85
8007	Miniature Metal Pullman Cars, Assorted Colors, 3 inches	.85
8008	Miniature Metal Locomotive, 3 inches	.85
8009	Miniature Metal Locomotive Coal Tender, 1½ inches	.42
2401	Enamelled Tape Measures, Assorted Colors, 1½ inches	1.90
2402	White Metal Tape Measures, 1½ inches	1.50
		GROSS
5730/118	Miniature White Metal Roller Skates, 1¾ inches	$1.80
8065	Miniature Bicycle with Colored Wheels, 1½ inches	1.20
		DOZEN
146/4	Miniature Metal Army Mule, 1½ inches	$.75
32/367	Metal Dogs, Painted, 2 inches	.80
368	White Metal Fireman's Helmet, 2½ inches	.90
31/801	Gilt Metal Pump, "The Old Village Pump," 4½ inches	1.05
31/800	Red Painted Metal Wheelbarrow, 4½ inches	.70
31/802	Red Painted Metal Hand Truck, 5½ inches	.90
31/804	White Painted Metal Paper Weight, "Don't Park Here," 4½ inches.	1.65
601/241	Grey Painted Metal Cannon, 1¾ inches	.30
8023	Miniature Metal Train Set, Engine, Coal Truck and Three Cars, Each Set in Box, 1 inch	.55
6999/W6	Miniature Wire Broiler, 6 inches	.60
32/329	Miniature Nickel Plated "Masonic" Trowl with Wooden Handle, Each in Box, Splendidly Made, 4 inches	$2.10

METAL NOVELTIES (Continued)
FRENCH METAL NOVELTIES IN ATTRACTIVE COLORS

29/103    792/202   6083/12

		DOZEN
601/200	Metal Bed, Pink, Blue and White, 3 inches	$.45
601/201	Metal High Chair, Pink, Blue and White, 3 inches	.45
601/204	Metal Baby Carriage, Pink, Blue and White, 2½ inches	.45
601/203	Metal Cradle, Pink, Blue and White, 2½ inches	.45
601/205	Metal Piano, Pink, Blue and White, 2½ inches	.45
601/202	Metal Parlor Chair, Pink, Blue and White, 2½ inches	.45
601/216	Metal Stoves, Pink, Blue and White, 2½ inches	.45

METAL BELLS

		GROSS
30/400	Gilt Metal Costume Bell, ½ inch	$1.00
30/401	Silver Metal Costume Bell, ½ inch	1.00
30/402	Gilt Metal Costume Bell, ¾ inch	1.25
30/403	Gilt Metal Open Bell, ⅝ inch	2.40
30/404	Silver Metal Open Bell, ⅝ inch	2.70
30/405	Gilt Metal Open Bell, ⅞ inch	3.50
30/406	Silver Metal Open Bell, ⅞ inch	3.75

METAL BASKETS

		PER 100
11803	Round Gilt Wire Basket, 1½ inches	$2.25
792/200	Round Gilt Wire Basket, 1½ inches	2.25
792/201	Round Silver Wire Basket, 1½ inches	2.25
792/202	Square Gilt Wire Basket, 2 inches	3.00
792/203	Square Silver Wire Basket, 2 inches	3.00
792/206	Round Gilt Wire Basket, 2¼ inches	4.50
792/207	Round Silver Wire Basket, 2¼ inches	4.50
392	Round Gilt Wire Basket, 3 inches	5.00
392S	Round Silver Wire Basket, 3 inches	5.00
346	Oval Gilt Wire Basket, 3 inches	6.00
792/20	Oval Gilt Wire Basket, 3½ inches	7.00
		DOZEN
309	Silver Filigree Wire Basket, Assorted Shapes, 3 inches	$1.95

METAL CANDLEHOLDERS

		GROSS
35/604	White Metal Candlestick, 1¾ inches	$2.40
35/605	White Metal Candelabra, Three Arms, 2½ inches	4.20
35/606	White Metal Candelabra, Five Arms, 2½ inches	6.60
601/206	Painted Metal Candelabra, Three Arms, 2 inches	3.60
90/715	Painted Metal Candelabra, Three Arms, 3 inches	5.40

29/103	Gilt Metal Cupid with Bow and Arrow, 2 inches	3.90
29/100	Gilt Metal Arrow, 3¾ inches	2.70
29/102	Gilt Metal Bow and Arrow, 2 inches	3.30
29/104	Gilt Metal Wishbone, 4 inches	4.20
29/105	Gilt Metal Horseshoe, 3¾ inches	5.40
		DOZEN
6083/12	Red Tin Wall Telephone, when crank is turned bell rings, 3 inches	$.90

MINIATURE WOOD NOVELTIES
A Wonderful Selling Line of Small Imported Wood Favors

30103   2539/47   2539/30

DOZEN

2909	Miniature Flower Wagon Filled with Assorted Flowers, 3¼ inches......	$.75
2908	Miniature Wood Auto Trucks, Filled with Barrels, Cases, etc., Assorted Colors and Styles, 2½ inches..............	.65
2907	Miniature Wood Wagons and Carts, Highly Polished, Assorted Styles and Colors in Box, 3¼ inches..............	.75
1616	Miniature Wood Racing Auto, Assorted Colors, 2½ inches........	.75
2924	Miniature Wood Fruit Stand with Woman, 2 inches..........	.80
30102	Miniature Wood Swing, 3 inches............	.45
2927	Miniature Wood Bird House on Stand with Bird, 3 inches........	.65
32/453	Miniature Wood Cradle, 1¾ inches..............	.65
2926	Miniature Wood See Saw with Two Figures, Nicely Colored, 2 inches...	.65
2906	Miniature Wood Coffee Mill, 1¼ inches............	.35
30601	Decorated Wood Ten Pin Set with Ball, Each Set in Box, 4¾ inches....	.70
32/472	Miniature Wood Barrel Filled with Toy Clothes Pins, 3 inches..........	.65
2913/488	Miniature White Wood Spinning Wheel, 3 inches........	.75
30109	Miniature White Wood Spinning Wheel, 5½ inches..............	1.20
30607	Miniature Wood Rocking Cradle, Assorted Colors, Nicely Decorated, 1½ inches..........	.60
2539/31	Miniature Wood Wobbling Duck on Wheels, Moves Head and Beak when Rolled, 2 inches..............	.80
2539/30	Same as 2539/31, but 3 inches..............	1.25
8051	Same as 2539/31, but 4 inches..............	1.90
2539/47	Miniature Wood Decorated Phonograph, 2½ inches..............	.70
2539/28	Miniature Wood Bird Cage with Assorted Color Birds, 1¾ inches........	1.50
50/101	Miniature Wood Old-Fashioned Baby Carriage with Handle, Attractive Colors, 4 inches..............	1.20
32/116	Miniature Wood Carts and Trucks, Assorted, 1¾ inches............	1.50
2539/92	Miniature Wood Open Wedding Carriage with Bride and Groom, 4 inches.	1.20
2929	Miniature Wood Market Stand, 1½ inches............	.60

MINIATURE NOVELTIES IN BOXES

DOZEN

30103	"The Smallest Kitchen in the World," Miniature Wood Farm Kitchen in Box, 2 inches.	$.45
A111	"The Smallest Sick Room in the World," 2 inches............	.45
32/121	"The Smallest Train Set in the World," 2 inches............	.45
E.31	"The Smallest Colonial Village in the World," 2 inches............	.45
7002	"The Smallest Building Blocks in the World," 2 inches............	.45
7028	"The Smallest Set Dominoes in the World," 2 inches............	.45
30106	"The Smallest Swine Herd in the World," 2 inches............	.42
2902	"The Smallest Xylophone in the World," 2 inches............	.45
30602	"The Smallest Box of Transfers in the World," 2 inches............	.45
32/120	"The Smallest Carpenter Shop in the World," 2 inches............	.45
2903	"The Smallest Lotto Game in the World," 2 inches............	.45
30107	"The Smallest Fighters in the World," 2 inches............	.45
30104	"The Smallest Workshop in the World," 2 inches............	.45
30105	"The Smallest Market Store in the World," 2 inches............	.45

All of the above items are nicely boxed in individual match boxes.

MINIATURE WOOD NOVELTIES (Continued)

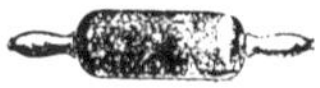

10535   2911   2539/92

		DOZEN
2539/62	Miniature Winter Figures on Skiis, 1½ inches	$.65
1611	Miniature Wood Bird on Base, 2½ inches	1.10
2539/88	Miniature Wood Tennis Racquet, 4 inches	.40
10535	Miniature White Wood Rolling Pin, 5 inches	.75
12515/31	Miniature Painted Merry-Go-Round with Animal and Figures, 3½ in.	2.40
2922	Miniature Painted Merry-Go-Round with Four Aeroplanes, 2½ inches.	1.20
2539/33	Painted Wood Kitchen Set Complete with Chairs, Tables, etc., 2½ in.	2.10
2923	Punch and Juddy Theatre, 3 inches	1.20
30603	Miniature White Wood Sled, 3 inches	.35
2913/2093	Miniature Painted Wood Orchestra on Stage; Numerous Players with Musical Instruments, Each Set in Box, 4 inches	5.40
2905	Miniature Wood Wine Set, Bottle with Four Goblets, Each Set in Box, 2¼ inches.	1.10
30108	Miniature Wood Farm Outhouse with Figure, 2 inches	.65
32/410	Miniature Wood Comic Figure Needle Case, 3½ inches	.75
30600	Miniature Painted Wooden Stork on Base, 1¾ inches	.42
2933	Miniature White Wood Sled, 4 inches	.60
2934	Miniature White Wood Sled, 6 inches	1.10
32/421	Miniature Wooden Pencil Box, Nicely Decorated, 2¾ inches	.35
2916	Miniature Painted Steam Roller, 3 inches	1.20
2539/58	Woman Washing Clothes in Tub Mounted on Platform, 2 inches	1.00
12515/49	Cat Running After Mouse, 3 inches	2.00
12515/50	Circus Wagon with Animals, 3 inches	2.20
7699/4	Comic Painted Figures Standing, 2 inches	.65
7017	Miniature Wooden Painted Banjo, 4 inches	.70
6578/28	Miniature Painted Auto Trucks, Assorted, Well Made, 2½ inches	1.70
6578/29	Miniature Painted Horse and Wagon, Assorted, Well Made, 2½ inches	1.70
1500	Miniature Painted Wooden Windmill, 2 inches	.60
30605	Miniature Dutch Farm Windmill, Nicely Decorated, 2¼ inches	.60
2935	Painted Windmill with Comic Moving Figure, 4 inches	.90

COMIC WOODEN FIGURES

		GROSS
2913	Painted Wooden Musician Figures, 12 Assorted Styles, 1½ inches	$4.50
2176	Painted Wooden Comic Tyrolean Figure, Movable Arms and Legs, 2 inches.	4.80
2174	Painted Wooden Comic Dressed Frog Figure, 2 inches	4.80
2165	Painted Wooden Comic Sailor Figure, 2 inches	4.80
2172	Painted Wooden Chauffeur Figure, 2 inches	4.80
2167	Painted Wooden Comic Darkie Boy Figure, 2 inches	4.80
8628/7	Painted Wooden Comic Dude Figure, 2½ inches	7.80
34409	Painted Wooden Comic Jumping Clown Figure, 3 inches	7.20
2913/657/1	Painted Wooden Woodsmen Figure, 2½ inches	9.60
13739	Painted Wooden Egg, Assorted Colors with Smallest Clown Figure	13.20

		DOZEN
30604	Painted Wooden Tumbling Clown Figure on Stand, 2½ inches	$.75
520/140	Painted Wooden Battleship, Each in Box, 3½ inches	.80
O7	Painted Wooden Steamship, 4 inches	.75
30100	Miniature Painted Sail and Steam Boats, Assorted to Box, 3 inches	.70
2544/4	Painted Wooden Racing Shell with Figure, 3½ inches	.85
D4	Painted Wooden Steamship, Each in Box, 5 inches	2.10
2937	White Wood Folding Steamer Chair, 7 inches	.35
628/0	Miniature Wooden Slate and Pencil Box with Book, 3 inches	1.25
C13	Miniature Wooden Trolley Car, 3 inches	.75
2911	Miniature Wooden Fire Engine, Hook and Ladder, etc., Assorted in Box, 2½ inches.	1.20

NOVELTY HAND CARVED AND PAINTED
ITALIAN WOOD FAVORS

48/214   48/204   48/216

		DOZEN
48/216	Wooden Birds Standing on Round Base. Beautiful Assorted Colors, 1½ inches.	.80
48/207	Wooden Comic Head Figure Pins, Splendidly Carved, 2 inches	1.00
48/202	Wooden Jointed Dolls with Pretty Assorted Color Satin Dresses, 1 in.	1.20
48/212	Wooden Jointed Dolls with Pretty Assorted Color Satin Peasant Dresses, 1¾ inches.	1.20
48/223	Wooden Eggs, Assorted Colors, Painted Floral Decorations with Small Wooden Jointed Baby Doll Inside, 1½ inches	1.20
48/213	Wooden Painted Comic Dogs with Glass Eyes, Assorted Colors, 2 in.	1.20
48/214	Gilded Wooden Dutch Pair of Shoes with Floral Decorations, Well Made, 1 inch.	1.25
48/215	Black Wooden Dutch Pair of Clogs with Hob Nails, 1 inch	1.25
48/203	Wooden Jointed Doll with Pretty Assorted Color Satin Colonial Dresses, 1½ inches.	1.50
48/217	Wooden Jointed Doll, Assorted Color Satin Clown Costumes, 2¼ in....	1.50
48/201	Wooden Comic Black Cat with Assorted Color Ribbon Bow, 2 inches	1.90
48/221	Same as 48/201 but size 3 inches	3.00
48/222	Same as 48/201 but size 4 inches	3.70
48/211	Wooden Baby Rocking Cradle, Assorted Colors with Pretty Floral Decoration and Tiny Wooden Baby under Satin Cover, 1⅛ in...	1.60
48/224	White Painted Wooden Stork on Round Base with Hollow Body, Containing Tiny Wooden, Jointed Baby Doll, Well Made, 3 in.	1.95
48/220	Wooden Rustic Barn with Sign "Stork Villa," Containing Small Painted Stork and Three Babies in Nest, Attractively Colored, 2¼ inches.	2.40
48/200	Wooden Painted Comic Happy Hooligan Figure with Three Small Happy Hooligan Figures Inside, Beautifully Colored, Well Made, 4 inches.	3.30
48/218	Wooden Comic Clown Figure with Movable Arms, Dressed in Attractive Assorted Color Satin Costumes, 4½ inches	6.00
48/204	Wooden Painted Doll with Movable Arms, Very Pretty Assorted Color Satin Dresses and Picture Hats Standing on Colored Wood Base, 2½ inches.	3.95
48/205	Wooden Painted Doll with Movable Arms, Very Pretty Assorted Color Satin Dresses and Picture Hats Standing on Satin Covered Wood Base, 5 inches	8.40
48/206	Wooden Painted Doll, Movable Arms with Attractively Frilled Colonial Style Assorted Color Dresses and Picture Hat Standing on Hand Painted Floral Decorated Wood Candy Box, 8 inches	27.00
48/208	Wooden Spoon with Painted Comic Figure Handles, 5 inches	1.65
48/209	Wooden Paper Cutter and Book Mark with Assorted Hand Carved and Painted Comic Figure Handle, 4½ inches	1.65
		DOZEN SETS
48/210	Wooden Spoon and Fork Salad Set with Assorted Hand Carved and Painted Comic Figure Handle, Splendidly Made, 10½ inches	$9.60
48/225	Wooden Hand Carved and Painted Comic Figure Novelty Nut Cracker, Very Strong and Well Made, 7¾ inches	DOZEN 12.60

MINIATURE WOOD NOVELTIES (Continued)
FURNITURE SETS

1630

32/29   50/100

		DOZEN
1615	White Wood Furniture Set, Table and Three Armchairs and Flower Pot, 1 inch.	$.90
1509	Miniature White Painted Wood Lawn Set, Table, Three Chairs and Settee, Each Set in Box, Each Piece About 1½ inches	.80
1504	Painted Blue Wood Porch Set, Table, Two Chairs and Settee, Each Piece About 1½ inches, Each Set in Box	.80
2921	Painted Blue Wood Breakfast Set, Table, Three Chairs and Settee, Each Piece About 1 inch, Each Set in Box	1.10
1630	Natural Color Wood Kitchen Set, Table and Three Chairs, Each Piece About 2½ inches, Each Set in Box	1.10
2920	White Wood Furniture Set, Table, Settee and Three Chairs, Each Set in Box.	.65
2919	White Painted Decorated Wood Furniture Set, Table, Settee and Two Chairs, Each Piece About 1 inch, Each Set to Box	.85
		GROSS
60/1040P	Natural Color Wood Painted Pig, Sheep, Cow and Goat, Assorted, 2½ inches.	$3.60
60/1041H	Natural Color Wood Painted Horse, 3½ inches	4.80
		DOZEN
110/1	Painted Comic Face Wooden Jumping Clown, 2 inches	$.70
200/6	Painted Comic Face, Carved Comic Figures, Assorted, 2 inches	.70
140/1/3	Painted Comic Face, Carved Comic Figures Swinging on Bar, 7 inches	.75
200/4	Painted Comic Face, Carved Wooden Clown Figure, Assorted, 2¼ inches.	1.00
250/5	Painted Comic Face, Wooden Clown Figure with Moving Head, Arms and Legs, Assorted, 5¼ inches.	1.60
2904	White Painted Wood Decorated Breakfast Set, Six Pieces to Set, Each Set in Box	1.70
		DOZEN
2262/1	Natural Color Wood Kitchen Cooking Set, Rolling Pin, Chopping Board, Chopper and Flour Box, etc., each piece about 2 inches, 7 pieces on card	$1.25
15042	Miniature Wood Beer Barrel on Stand, Nicely Colored, 3½ inches	1.35
11312	Painted Musical Bird Warbler on Wooden Base, Nicely Colored, 3 inches.	1.25
32/29	Wood Baseball Bat, Bright Finish, Can Be Filled, 15 inches	2.00
32/251	Painted Wood Stork with Baby Carriage, Each Set in Box, 2½ inches	1.10
2917	Miniature Wooden Train Set, Locomotive and Three Cars, Each Set in Box, 5½ inches.	1.80
2918	Miniature Wooden Train Set, Locomotive, Three Cars, Each Set in Box, each piece about 1¾ inches	1.90
		DOZEN
50/100	Wooden Swan and Duck Boat on Wheels, Nicely Colored, 3 inches	1.35
6095/619/0	Wooden Handle Dust Pan Brush, 2½ inches	.30
2936	Wooden Jointed Wriggling Snake, 21 inches	.85
60/1013/0	Wooden Jointed Wriggling Snake, Well Made, 22 inches	1.00
32/3	Wooden Bubble Pipe "Junior," Each in Box, 3½ inches	.30
32/4	Wooden Bubble Pipe "Multiple," Each in Box, 5 inches	.65

CELLULOID NOVELTIES
These Novelties Are Well Made of Extra Heavy Celluloid and Nicely Colored.

X4174   34/108   68/4

		DOZEN
31/300	Celluloid Parasols, Assorted Colors, 2½ inches	$.70
31/301	Celluloid Parasols, Assorted Colors, 3½ inches	.85
31/304	Celluloid Vase on Stand, Assorted Colors, 2¾ inches	.90
31/305	Celluloid Bird Cage with Bird, Assorted Colors, 2 inches	1.00
130	Celluloid Miniature House, Assorted Colors, 2½ inches	.90
136	Celluloid Beer Keg on Stand, Assorted Colors, 2½ inches	1.10
137	Celluloid Wheelbarrow, Assorted Colors, 4 inches	.90
138	Celluloid Kiddie Car, Assorted Colors, 3 inches	.90
8838	Celluloid Folding Fan, White Only, 3 inches	.75
X4174	Celluloid Folding Fan, White Only, 5½ inches	1.90
68/48	Celluloid Blue Bird, 3½ inches	1.25
68/4	Celluloid Canary Whistle, 3½ inches	.80

CELLULOID BIRD PLACE CARD HOLDERS

		GROSS
34/100	Celluloid Balancing Blue Bird Card Holder with Card, 3½ inches	$4.50
34/102	Celluloid Balancing Red Bird Card Holder with Card, 3½ inches	4.50
34/103	Celluloid Balancing Yellow Bird Card Holder with Card, 3½ inches	4.50
34/104	Celluloid Balancing Pink Bird Card Holder with Card, 3½ inches	4.50
34/105	Celluloid Balancing Green Bird Card Holder with Card, 3½ inches	4.50
34/106	Celluloid Balancing White Bird Card Holder with Card, 3½ inches	4.50
34/108	Celluloid Balancing Parrot Card Holder, Assorted Colors, 3½ in	4.50
38/702	Celluloid Balancing Parrot, 5 inches	12.00
34/109	Celluloid Balancing Monkey Place Card Holder, Very Distinctive Novelty, 3¾ inches	8.40

CELLULOID DOLLS

		DOZEN
3560/6	White Celluloid Sitting Doll, 1½ inches	$.70
3560/5B	Black Celluloid Sitting Doll, 1 inch	.40
3560/5W	White Celluloid Sitting Doll, 1 inch	.40
2748/10B	Black Celluloid Standing Kewpie, 2½ inches	.90
2748/8B	Black Celluloid Standing Kewpie, 3 inches	1.30
		GROSS
8061	White Celluloid Doll on Pin, 1 inch	$1.50
520/173	White Celluloid Standing Doll, Movable Arms, 2½ inches	4.50
520/173/5	White Celluloid Doll, Movable Arms and Legs, 2½ inches	4.20
4034	White Celluloid Doll, Movable Arms and Legs, 3½ inches	5.40
		DOZEN
2748/10	White Celluloid Standing Kewpie, 2½ inches	$1.20
2748/80W	White Celluloid Standing Kewpie, 3¼ inches	1.50
520/263	White Celluloid Standing Doll with Movable Arms, 3½ inches	.55
8080	White Celluloid Standing Doll with Movable Arms, 5 inches	1.25
6409/600	White Celluloid Standing Doll with Movable Arms, 6 inches	1.50
2075/3835	White Celluloid Sitting Doll, Nicely Dressed with Knitted Dress, Hat and Socks, 3¼ inches	2.25

CELLULOID NOVELTIES (Continued)
CELLULOID ANIMALS

64/18   29604   68/120

		DOZEN
29604	Celluloid Animals, Assorted, 2 inches	$.70
64/63	Celluloid Camel, 3¼ inches	1.20
64/18	Celluloid "King Tut" Camel, Nicely Painted, 2¼ inches	.70
64/68	Celluloid "King Tut" Camel, Nicely Painted, 3¼ inches	1.25
32/379	Celluloid Natural Color Elks, 2¼ inches	.50
32/380	Celluloid Natural Color Camel, 2¼ inches	.50
29600	Celluloid Novelty Paper Cutter, Alligator with Nigger in Mouth, 3¾ inches	.70
29601	Celluloid Novelty Paper Cutter, Alligator with Nigger Headed Pencil in Mouth, 5¼ inches	1.90
35/146	Celluloid Novelty Alligator Paper Cutter, 4½ inches	.85
15/100	Celluloid Novelty Alligator Paper Cutter, 7¼ inches	1.25
2	Celluloid Turtle on Wheels, 2¾ inches	2.20
4	Celluloid Comic Clown on Wheels, 3 inches	2.20
1	Celluloid Boat on Wheels, 4½ inches	2.20
14895	Celluloid Turkey Place Card Holder with Place Card, 2¼ inches	1.65
35/145	Celluloid Circus Seal with Ball, 3¼ inches	.70
14899	Celluloid Birds, Assorted Colors, 2½ inches	.85
14805	White Celluloid Nodding Goose, 2¾ inches	.80
32/311	Celluloid Comic Dressed Man Rabbit Figures, 4 inches	.38

CELLULOID COMIC ROLY POLIES

Well made of heavy celluloid, highly colored.

		DOZEN
13503	Celluloid Roly Poly, Assorted Comic Figures, 1½ inches	$.42
14838	Celluloid Roly Poly, Assorted Comic Figures with Large Heads, 2 inches	.60
13501	Celluloid Roly Poly, Assorted Animals, 2¼ inches	.65
13500	Celluloid Alligator Roly Poly, 2¼ inches	.65
19187/1	Celluloid Chicken Roly Poly, 2¾ inches	.80
19187/2	Celluloid Clown Roly Poly, 3½ inches	.80

CELLULOID RATTLES

		DOZEN
13505	Celluloid Rattles, Assorted Comic Children, 4 inches	$.80
13506	Celluloid Rattle with Striped Colored Ball Top, 6 inches	1.45
13504	Celluloid Stork Rattle, 6½ inches	1.75
14861	Celluloid Bird Rattles, Assorted Colors, Well Made, 5 inches	1.90
35/134	Celluloid Man and Woman Rabbit Rattles, 6 inches	1.90
14859	Celluloid Dog Rattle, Standing Positions, 2½ inches	.75
14860	Celluloid Bird Rattles, Assorted Colors, 2½ inches	.80
566/921	Celluloid Comic Figure Rattles, 3½ inches	.65
71398/402	Celluloid Chicken Rattle, 2¾ inches	.45
4005	Celluloid Comic Figure Rattles with Assorted Vegetable Heads, 3½ inches	.45
35/131	Celluloid Rattles, Assorted Sheep, Chicken and Rabbits with Cart, 3¾ inches	.85
35/119	Celluloid Comic Boot with Chick Rattle, 5½ inches	2.05

CELLULOID NOVELTIES (Continued)

| 6224/65 | 14817 | 50/31 | 601/22 |

FLOATING TOYS

		DOZEN
14815	Celluloid Floating Animals, Ducks, Frogs, Swans, Turtles, Assorted Colors, 1 dozen to box, 1½ inches	$.30
14816	Celluloid Floating Animals, Medium Size, Ducks, Frogs, Swans, Turtles, Assorted Colors, 1 dozen to box, 2 inches	.35
14817	Celluloid Floating Animals, Large Size, Ducks, Frogs, Swans, Turtles, Assorted Colors, 1 dozen to box, 2¾ inches	.65
		DOZEN SETS
14834	Celluloid Floating Animals in Net, Assorted Colors, Swans, Ducks, Frogs, Turtles, etc., 6 in net, 2 inches	2.20
		DOZEN
14828	Celluloid Floating Animals, Ducks, Frogs, Swans, Turtles, Assorted Colors, 12 to box, 3 inches	$1.25
14844	Celluloid Bathtubs, Assorted Colors, Small Doll in Each Tub, 12 to box, 1½ inches	.35
14846	Celluloid Bathtubs, Assorted Colors, Small Doll in Each Tub, 12 to box, 3 inches	.80

CELLULOID DOLL TOILET AND BATH SETS

		DOZEN
35/124	Celluloid Doll Brush and Comb Set, in Box, 3¼ inches	$2.00
50/31	Celluloid Doll Brush, Comb and Mirror Set, In Box, 5 inches	4.00
14851	Celluloid Doll Toilet Set, Brush, Comb, Mirror, Sponge and Soap, Each Set in Box, 3x5 inches	3.00
6224/24	Celluloid Doll Toilet Set, Brush and Comb, Each Set in Box, 3x2¼ inches	1.00
6224/20	Celluloid Doll Toilet Set, Brush, Comb and Mirror, Each Set in Box, 3½x3 inches	2.10
15923	Celluloid Doll Toilet Set, Brush, Mirror, Two Combs, Sponge, Soap Tray and Towel, Each Set in Box, 5½x4¼ inches	3.90
20463	Celluloid Doll Toilet Set, Nursing Bottle, Mirror, Sponge, Doll and Soap Tray, Each Set in Box, 3x4 inches	1.00
		DOZEN
14844	Celluloid Doll in Bath Tub, Assorted Colors, 12 to Box, 1¼ inches	$.35
6224/65	Miniature Celluloid Hand Mirror, 3¼ inches	.70
6224/53	Miniature Celluloid Toilet Mirror, 2 inches	.70
6999/37	Celluloid Round Mirror, 1½ inches	.75
6999/183	Miniature Celluloid Hand Mirror, 4 inches	1.10
6999/187	Brown Celluloid Oblong Mirror, 2½ inches	.70

NOVELTY DOLL SPECTACLES

68/120	Miniature Celluloid Imitation Tortoise Shell Doll Spectacles, 2½ inches	.60
601/22	Miniature Doll Lorgnette, Well Made, Each in Box, 4x1¾ inches	2.40
68/45	Celluloid Dishes with Imitation Fruits, Cake, Meat, etc., 2½ inches	1.20

GLASS NOVELTIES AND FAVORS

275/1058    11870    2000

GLASS NURSING BOTTLES AND FLOWER POTS

		GROSS
32/221	Glass Nursing Bottle with Rubber Tip in Knitted Bag, 2¼ inches	$4.20
3182/48	Glass Nursing Bottle with Rubber Tip in Knitted Bag, 3 inches	6.00
3182/51	Glass Nursing Bottle with Rubber Tip in Knitted Bag, 3½ inches	8.40
15983	Glass Nursing Bottle with Rubber Tip, 2 inches	3.60
3556/5	Clouded Glass Nursing Bottle with Rubber Tip, 3½ inches	4.20
6742/13	Glass Nursing Bottle with Rubber Tip, 2½ inches	3.60
15982	Glass Nursing Bottle and Miniature Pacifier, on Card, 4 inches	4.50
15985	Glass Nursing Bottle with Rubber Tip and Tube, Each in Box, 3¾ inches	4.20
15984	Nursing Bottle Set, Bottle with Rubber Tube and Tip, Miniature Rattle and Pacifier, Each Set in Box, 3¾ inches	8.40
13714	Nursing Set, Clouded Glass Nursing Bottle with Rubber Tip, Miniature Rattle and Pacifier, Each Set in Box, 4¾x3½ inches	12.00

		DOZEN
2000	Glass Flower Pot with Assorted Linen Flowers, 2 inches	$.35
8402	Glass Flower Pot with Assorted Linen Rose Sprays, 3 inches	.90
8406	Fancy Glass Flower Pot with Assorted Linen Rose Sprays, 4 inches	2.70
275/1057	Decorated Glass Flower Vase with Violets and Ferns, 3 inches	.42
275/1058	Decorated Glass Flower Vase with Assorted Flowers, 3½ inches	.70
275/1060	Colored Glass Flower Vase with Linen Roses and Leaves, 5 inches	1.20

		PER 100
32/1	Fluted Glass Candlestick with Handle, 1 inch	$3.50
32/2	Fluted Glass Candlestick with Handle, 1¾ inches	8.00

		DOZEN
8404	Glass Clock with Movable Hands, 1 inch	.70
8405	Glass Dog on Round Base, 1¼ inches	2.40
1676/0	Glass Vanity Box, Hinged Lid with Four Leaf Clover Design and Mirror, 1¼ inches.	3.30

GLASS BOTTLES AND WINE SETS

		GROSS
21100	Glass Miniature Liquor Bottles Containing Colored Liquid, 2 inches	$3.60
11851	Glass Miniature Liquor Bottles Containing Colored Liquid, 2¼ inches	4.20
11849	Miniature Glass Long Neck Wine Bottle, 2 inches	4.20
5545	Glass Miniature Liquor Bottle, Assorted Shapes and Colors	7.80
5546	Glass Miniature Liquor Flask Containing Colored Liquid, 1¾ inches	9.00
21104	Miniature Glass Water Bottle with Tumbler, 2 inches	9.60
11898	Glass Miniature Liquor Bottle Containing Colored Liquid, 12 Assorted Shapes and Colors to Box	7.20
11889	Glass Miniature Flower Vase, Assorted Color and Design, 2½ inches	4.80
11892	Glass Miniature Assorted Bottles, Jugs and Goblets, 1½ inches	4.80
11882	Glass Miniature Assorted Bottles, Jugs and Goblets, 2¼ inches	5.40

		DOZEN SETS
21106	Glass Wine Set, Decanter, Glasses and Tray, 4 inches	$3.30
11870	Glass Wine Set, Bottle with Colored Liquid, Two Glasses and Tray, 1½ inches.	1.00
21105	Glass Wine Set, Decanter with Colored Liquid, Three Glasses and Tray, 2½ inches.	2.40

		DOZEN
11850	Glass Wine Goblets Filled with Colored Liquid, 1¼ inches	$.30
11899	Glass Wine Goblets, Nicely Decorated, 1¼ inches	.35
21101	Glass Wine Jug, Nicely Decorated, 1½ inches	.65

CHINA FAVORS AND NOVELTIES

| 1433/9 | 1433/6 | 1433/5 |

DOZEN

1433/10	White China Cupid with Bow and Arrow, Kneeling on China Heart, 2½ inches.	$2.40
1433/1	China Cupid with Heart and Ring, 2½ inches	2.25
1433/3	Gold China Slipper, 1½ inches	1.10
1433/7	Gold China Ring with Dove, 1½ inches	1.00
1433/8	Gold China Horseshoe with Dove, 1½ inches	1.00
1433/9	White China Cupid, Sitting, 1½ inches	.75
1433/2	Double Gold China Wedding Rings with Two Doves, 2½ inches	1.80
1433/5	Double Gold China Slipper with Two Doves, 2 inches	1.80
1433/4	Gold China Key, 2¼ inches	1.30
1433/13	China Cupid Holding Gold Wedding Ring, 2 inches	1.80
1433/6	Gold China Heart with Two White Doves, 1½ inches	1.80
1433/14	China Nest with Two White Doves and Tiny Gold Ring, 2 inches	1.80
1433/12	White China Cupid with Slipper, 1¾ inches	1.60
1433/11	White China Cupid Sitting on Large Gold Wedding Ring, 2½ inches.	2.60
1433/15	China Cupid with Wedding Ring and Dove Sitting on China Trunk, 2½ inches.	3.60
1433/100	White China Cupid, 12 Assorted Positions and Designs to Box, each about 2 inches.	2.10
1211/2879	White China Cupid Sitting with White Dove on Knee, 2½ inches	1.95
1211/2880	White China Cupid with Anvil Dove and Two Wedding Rings, 3 inches.	2.70
1206	White China Cupid Holding Wedding Ring, 2 inches	4.20
2/1556/23	Colored Glazed China Cupid Holding Wedding Rings and Hearts, Well Made, 2 inches.	4.50

| 1433/11 | | 1433/10 |

DOZEN

1433/47	China Cupid Holding Letter Sitting in China Auto, 2½ inches	$2.50
12726	White China Cupid with Two Hearts on String, 2 inches	3.00
12728	White China Cupid with Open China Bowl, 2 inches	2.70
1210	China Cupid Glazed Flesh Color with Assorted Musical Instruments, 2 inches.	5.40
12741	Flesh Color China Cupid Playing with Two Hearts, 1½ inches	2.25
1433/45	Gilt China Double Slipper, 1½ inches	1.70
1433/56	Gilt China Violin with Dove, 1¾ inches	1.50
12753	White China Swan with Baby, 2 inches	1.50

CHINA FAVORS AND NOVELTIES (Continued)
CHINA NOVELTY KEWPIE DOLLS

		DOZEN
55/C	China Kewpie Doll, Standing, Movable Arms, 4½ inches	$2.00
38	China Kewpie Doll with Black Cat on Lap, 3¼ inches	2.20
36	China Kewpie Doll, Assorted Comic Positions, 4 inches	2.20
35	China Kewpie Doll with Dog on Lead, 3½ inches	4.20
37	China Kewpie Doll, Lovers, Two Dolls in Embrace, 3¾ inches	3.75
36B	China Kewpie Doll with Bag and Umbrella, 3½ inches	3.00
297/0	China Kewpie Doll, Standing Position, 5½ inches	4.20
297/2	China Kewpie Doll, Standing Position 7, inches	6.90
297/4	China Kewpie Doll, Standing Position, 8¾ inches	8.40
297/6	China Kewpie Doll, Standing Position, 12 inches	15.00

11L25   12770   36

CHINA DOLLS, COMIC POSITIONS

		DOZEN
12721	China Baby Doll, Sitting Position, 3½ inches	$5.40
12703	China Baby Doll with China Basket, Assorted Positions, 4 inches	4.50
1013	China Baby Doll, Dressed with Large Open China Basket, 3 inches	3.90
12704	China Baby Girl Doll Holding Yellow China Chick, 3 inches	5.40
1015	China Twin Baby Figures, Boy and Girl, Dressed, 3½ inches	9.00
12720	China Dutch Baby Doll, Sitting Position, 3½ inches	5.40
12715	China Twin Baby Dolls, Comic Positions, 4 inches	7.80
12713	China Doll Figure with China Watering Can and Flower Pot, 4½ in.	7.80
10211/4	China Doll Comic Position with Crochet Cap, 6 inches	13.20
12767	China Dutch Boy on Stand, Shaking, 3¼ inches	5.40
12768	China Dutch Girl on Stand, Shaking, 3¼ inch	5.40
12765	China Colonial Man Figure, Shaking, 3¼ inches	5.40
12766	China Colonial Lady Figure, Shaking, 3¼ inches	5.40
12775	China Colonial Girl Figure with Bell in Skirt, 3¼ inches	6.00
12770	Comic China Radio Kid, 2¼ inches	2.70
12771	Comic China Boy and Girl Figure, Place Card Holder, 2 inches	1.25
12774	Comic China Girl Doll Looking in Mirror, 2 inches	1.65
12772	Comic China Doll Holding Red Rose, 2 inches	1.65
12773	Comic China Doll with Banjo, 2 inches	1.65
1043	Comic China Boy and Girl Figure with Flower Moving Head, 3 in....	1.00
1044	Comic China Girl Figure with Flower and Movable Head, 3½ inches	1.40
1055	China Colonial Girl Figure with Decorated Skirt Covering White China Bowl which Can Be Filled, 3 inches	3.60
12777	Comic China Pup with Radio Set, Receiver and Head Piece, 3½ in	3.75
10043	Comic China Figures, "Dinty Moore," 3½ inches	2.10
10056	Comic China Figures, "Katzenjammer Kids," 3 inches	2.10
10045	Comic China Figures, "Happy Hooligans," 3 inches	2.10
10042	Comic China Figures, "Mutt," 4 inches	2.10
10044	Comic China Figures, "Jeff," 3 inches	2.10
10052	Comic China Figures, "Jiggs," 3 inches	2.10
10053	Comic China Figures, "Maggie," 3 inches	2.10

FLORAL DECORATED BASKETS AND NOVELTIES

	13827	13821	13800

		DOZEN
13830	Round China Basket with Handle, Decorated with Flowers, 2 inches..	$1.50
13800	Oval China Basket with Handles Decorated with Flowers, 3 inches......	3.25
13823	Round China Basket with Handles Decorated with Flowers, 2 inches....	3.25
13824	Fancy China Basket with Handles Decorated with Flowers, 3 inches....	3.25
13816	Open China Tray, Decorated with Flowers, 2¾ inches...........................	3.25
13810	China Basket, Kettle Shape, Decorated with Flowers, 1¾ inches..........	3.25
13807	China Slipper, Decorated with Flowers, 3 inches.................................	3.25
13808	China Swan with Opening, Decorated with Flowers, 2¾ inches...........	3.25
13821	Old-Fashion China Candlestick, Decorated with Flowers, 2¾ inches...	3.25
13806	China Sprinkling Can, Decorated with Flowers, 2¾ inches....................	3.25
13805	China Teapot with Cover, Decorated with Flowers, 2½ inches..............	3.25
13809	China Flower Vase with Handles, Decorated with Flowers, 2½ in......	3.25
13822	Round China Flower Vase, Decorated with Flowers, 3 inches...............	3.25
13831	White China Flower Vase, Decorated with Flowers, 3½ inches...........	2.70
13827	China Tea Kettle with Cover, Decorated with Flowers, 3 inches.........	5.40
13828	China Flower Vases with Handles, Decorated with Flowers, 3 inches.	5.40
13802	Round China Basket with Handles, Decorated with Flowers, 3 inches	5.40
13803	Square China Basket with Handles, Decorated with Flowers, 2½ inches	5.40
13826	Fancy China Basket with Handles, Decorated with Flowers, 4 inches	5.40
13825	China Bon Bon Dish with Cover, Decorated with Flowers, 3 inches....	5.40
13829	China Eggs with Opening, Decorated with Flowers, 3 inches...............	2.70
13819	China Egg on Bowl, Removable Cover, Decorated with Flowers, 4 in.	5.40
13832	China Rabbit with Open Egg, Decorated with Flowers, 4 inches.........	3.25

CHINA DOLLS

No. 1

		DOZEN
75/6	China Doll with Movable Arms, 2¼ inches..	$.75
90211	China Doll with Movable Arms with Painted Wig, 5 inches..................	1.10
10808	Dressed China Doll with Movable Arms and Legs, 3½ inches..............	1.35
1	China Dolls with Satin Dress, Movable Arms and Legs, 3 inches..........	1.50
12/1	China Doll with Movable Arms and Legs, Sleeping Eyes and Hair Wig, 4½ inches.	2.25
1054	China Doll, Colored Girl with Lace Dress and Ribbon Bow, 2¼ inches	1.25
1048	China Doll, White Girl with Lace Dress and Ribbon Bow, 2¼ inches	1.00
1049	China Doll, Girl Figure with Lace Skirt and Movable Arm, 2½ inches	1.50
725/379	China Doll with Bobbed Hair, Movable Arms and Legs, 3½ inches....	1.70
1051	China Doll with Movable Arms and Legs, Lace Dress, 5 inches...........	2.60

CHINA NOVELTIES (Continued)

1000   1010

COMIC CHINA FIGURES

		DOZEN
13307	Comic China Boy and Girl Kissing "The Great Lover," 3½ inches......	$5.40
13309	Comic China Stout Girl with Red Bathing Suit, 4½ inches...............	5.40
13320	Comic China Cat and Mouse on Ashtray, "I Get You Yet," 3½ inches	5.40
13305	Comic China Gay Sailor Sitting with Whiskey Bottle, 3 inches.............	5.40
13322	Comic China Baby with Open Mouth in Cradle (Ash Tray), 3 inches.	5.40
13303	Comic China Baby Girl with Dog Sitting on Box, 3½ inches...............	5.40
13310	Comic China Cupid Looking Through Keyhole, "At Last Alone," 5 inches.	5.40
13323	Comic China Stout Man, with Big Cigar, Sitting in Chair, "Mr. Bull," 4 inches.	5.40
13319	Comic China Man with Crying Baby, "That Is a Life," 4 inches...........	5.40
13300	Comic China Chef with Large Lobster, 5 inches...........	5.40
13304	Comic China Black Cat with Candle Shaped Tail. Can be used as an oil lamp, 5 inches.	5.40
13302	Comic China Baby Girl with Basket, 3½ inches...............	5.40
13312	Comic China Negro with Long Face, "Read Them and Weep," 3½ inches.	5.40
13318	Comic China Boy with Derby and Cigar, "His First Cigar," 4½ inches	5.40
13308	Comic China Men Lighting Cigar, "Couple of Stinkers," 4 inches.......	5.40
13321	Comic China Lady in Twin Beds, "All By Myself in the Morning," 4½ inches.	5.40
22G	Miniature White China Chamber Pot, Gilt Lined with Motto, 1½ inches.	.70
6G	Miniature White China Chamber Pot, Gilt Lined with Motto, 2⅛ inches.	1.50
7011	Miniature White China Toilet, with Modern Cover, 2¼ inches...............	1.10
1014/1006	Miniature Beer Stein with Assorted Mottoes, 1¼ inches.........................	.45

COMIC CHINA INDIAN DOLLS

		DOZEN
73/9	Comic Indian Doll with Red Feather, 3½ inches.....................................	$2.10
73/11	Comic Indian Doll with Red Feather, 4½ inches.....................................	3.30
73/14	Comic Indian Doll with Red Feather, 5½ inches.....................................	4.80
1061	China Dancing Indian Girl on Base, 6¼ inches....................................	7.20

MINIATURE CHINA TEA SETS

		DOZEN SETS
520/191	Decorated China Coffee Set, Coffee Pot, Cream Jug and Two Cups and Saucers with Tray, Each Set in Box, each piece about 1 inch.	$3.50
1701	Miniature Decorated China Tea Set, Tea Pot, Sugar Bowl and Creamer, Two Cups and Saucers on China Tray, each piece about 1 inch.	8.40
1709	Miniature Gold China Tea Set, Tea Pot, Sugar Bowl and Creamer, Two Cups and Saucers on Gold China Tray, each piece about 1 inch.	9.60
300/590	Decorated China Toilet Set, Water Jug, Wash Basin, Soap Dish and Chamber, each piece 1¼ inches.	4.00
520/230	Blue China Tea Set, Tea Pot, Cream Jug, Sugar Bowl, Two Cups and Saucers, each piece about 1½ inches.	4.20
520/231	Same as 520/230 but Yellow China...	4.20

CHINA NOVELTIES (Continued)

1709

CHINA ESKIMO FIGURES

		DOZEN
1000	White China Snow Babies, Assorted Positions, 1¼ inches	$.70
1001	White China Snow Babies on Skiis, 1½ inches	1.30
1002	White China Snow Babies Sitting on Sled, 1½ inches	1.50
1003	White China Twin Snow Babies Sitting on Sled, 2½ inches	2.40
1004	White China Snow Babies Sitting on Sled, 3¼ inches	2.25
1005	White China Snow Babies Lying on Sled, 3¼ inches	2.70
1006	White China Snow Babies, Assorted Positions, 3 inches	2.00
1039	White China Snow Babies, Sitting Positions, 3½ inches	3.90
1042	White China Snow Babies on Skiis, Assorted Positions, 3½ inches	3.90
1038	Colored China Snow Babies with Movable Heads, Sitting on White China Sled, 3¼ inches	2.70
1040	Colored China Twin Snow Babies Sitting on Sled, 3½ inches	3.90
1041	Colored China Twin Snow Babies with Movable Heads, Standing on Skiis Mounted on China Base, 3½ inches	4.50

10702    10706    10705

MINIATURE CROCHET DRESSED CHINA DOLLS AND ANIMALS

All hand made and have movable arms and legs

		DOZEN
12245/1	White China Doll Baby Dresses, Assorted Colors, 1¼ inches	$1.10
12245/2	Black China Doll Baby Dresses, Assorted Colors, 1¼ inches	.80
12245/153	White China Doll Full Knitted Dress, 1¼ inches	1.50
12747/117	White China Doll, Bride's and Groom's Cotton Suits and Dresses, 1¾ inches.	.85
12747/123	White China Swiss Boy and Girl Dolls, 1¾ inches	1.00
12747/124	White China Doll Dressed as Maid, 1¾ inches	.75
12747/125	White China Doll Dressed as Chef, 1¾ inches	.90
10700	White China Doll Bride, 1½ inches	2.10
10701	White China Doll Groom, 1½ inches	2.10
10706	White China Doll Chauffeur, 1½ inches	2.10
10707	White China Dolls, Assorted Dutch Boy and Girl, 1½ inches	1.80
10708	White China Doll Dressed as Football Player, 1½ inches	1.80
10709	White China Doll Dressed as Santa Claus, 1½ inches	2.20
10710	White China Doll Dressed as Snow Man, 1½ inches	1.60
10711	White China Doll Dressed as Rabbit, 1½ inches	2.10
10716	White China Doll Dressed as Sailor Boy, 1½ inches	1.60
725/376	White China Doll, Assorted Boy and Girl Dresses, 1½ inches	1.60
9815	White China Doll, Assorted Boy and Girl Dresses, 1½ inches	.65
10702	Crochet Animals, Teddy Bear, Nicely Colored, 1½ inches	2.10
10703	Crochet Animals, Dog, Nicely Colored, 1½ inches	2.10
10704	Crochet Animals, Elephant, Nicely Colored, 1½ inches	2.10
10705	Crochet Animals, Monkey, Nicely Colored, 1½ inches	2.10

CHINA NOVELTIES (Continued)

China Bathing Girl Figures with Wigs and Silk Bathing Suits and Hats Well Made. Life-like in Form and Expression.

| | 12750 | 1407 | 17413 | |

1407	China Bathing Girls, 12 Assorted Positions, with Attractive Suits and Hats, 5 inches	DOZEN $12.60
17409	China Bathing Girls, Standing Position on Velvet Pedestal, 4½ inches	13.20
1211/2806	China Bathing Girls, Assorted Positions, 6¼ inches	25.20
17404	China Bathing Girls, Reclining Position, Reading Book, 7 inches	25.20
1211/2811	China Bathing Girls, Standing Position, on China Base, 6 inches	18.00
17408	China Bathing Girls, Standing Position, on China Base, with Painted Stockings, 9 inches	34.00
17400	China Bathing Girls in China Canoe, Assorted Positions, 5½ inches	16.20
1211/2825	Two China Bathing Girls, One Sitting, One Standing, Assorted Poses, 4 inches	25.20
17406	Two China Bathing Girls, One Sitting, One Standing, Assorted Poses, 5 inches	28.80

ARTISTIC CHINA NUDE WOMAN FIGURES

12750	China Nude Woman Figure, Sitting Position, Flesh Color, Painted Wig, 2 inches	DOZEN $3.25
1018	Same as 12750 but assorted positions, 4 inches	5.40
1016	Same as 1017 but assorted positions, 5 inches	10.20
1011	China Nude Woman Figures, Assorted Positions, Painted Wig and Stockings, Flesh Color, 5½ inches	16.20
1012	Same as 1011 with Lace Underwear, 5½ inches	22.80
12746	China Nude Woman Figure, Assorted Positions, Painted Stockings and Natural Hair Wig, 4 inches	18.00
12748	Same as 12746 but 4¾ inches and better made	30.00
1022	White China Nude Woman Figure, Assorted Positions, 3½ inches	3.90
1017	Same as 1022 but 4½ inches	7.20
10097	China Nude Woman Figure, 3½ inches	$3.60
10091	China Nude Woman Figure, 4½ inches	5.40

ARTISTIC CHINA DANCING GIRL FIGURES

17413	China Dancing Girl Figure with China Lace Skirt and Natural Hair Wig, Assorted Positions, Well Made, 2½ inches	DOZEN $24.00
17410	China Dancing Girl Figure with Silk Lace Skirt and Natural Hair Wig, Assorted Positions, 3 inches	25.20
17411	China Dancing Girl Figure with Silk Lace Skirt and Natural Hair Wig, Assorted Positions, 4 inches	28.80
12755	China Dancing Girl Figure with Silk Lace Skirt and Natural Hair Wig, Assorted Positions, 5 inches	30.00

ARTISTIC COMPOSITION NUDE WOMAN FIGURES

Well Made, Perfect Form in Flesh Color, Natural Hair Wigs.

7009	Standing Nude Woman Figure on Base, 8 inches	DOZEN $19.80
7002	Same as 7009 but 9½ inches	25.20
7003	Same as 7009 but 10½ inches	27.00
7011	Nude Woman Figure Kneeling on Base, 6½ inches	24.00

77

CHINA NOVELTIES (Continued)
CHINA ANIMAL FAMILY SETS

1433/30

DOZEN SETS

1433/27	China Fox Terrier Family, Large Dog with Four Little Fox Terriers, each about 1¼ inches	$3.60
1433/30	China Cat Family, Cat and Four Kittens, each about 1¼ inches	3.60
1433/49	China Donkey Family, Donkey and Four Baby Donkeys, each about 1¼ inches.	3.60
1433/35	China Rabbit Family, Rabbit and Four Baby Rabbits, each about 1¼ inches.	3.60
1433/17	China Monkey Family, Monkey and Four Baby Monkies, each about 1¼ inches.	3.60
1433/34	China Elephant Family, Elephant and Four Baby Elephants, each about 1¼ inches.	3.60
1433/29	China Camel Family, Camel and Four Baby Camels, each about 1¼ inches.	3.60
1433/19	China Squirrel Family, Squirrel and Four Baby Squirrels, each about 1¼ inches.	3.60

MINIATURE HAND PAINTED CHINA VASES
DOZEN

4630/1	China Vase, Nicely Decorated, Six Assorted Shapes and Designs, 2 inches.	$2.60
4630/2	China Vase, Nicely Decorated, Six Assorted Shapes and Designs, 2½ inches.	3.60
4630/2/5	China Vase, Nicely Decorated, Six Assorted Designs, 3 inches	4.00
601/861	China Vase, Nicely Decorated, Six Assorted Shapes and Designs, 1½ inches.	4.20
601/863	China Chamber with Handle, Six Assorted Designs, ½ inch	4.20
4232/22	Decorated China Flower Pot with Miniature China Flowers, 2 inches	6.60
4232/26	Decorated Oval China Flower Pot with Miniature China Flowers and Ferns, 2½ inches.	12.00
100	Decorated Glass Flower Vase, 12 Assorted Designs, 2½ inches	1.95
101	Decorated Glass Flower Vase, 12 Assorted Designs, 3½ inches	3.40

AMERICAN FLAGS
GROSS

520/128	Silk Flag, Bow on Pin, 1½ inches	$1.20
520/127	Silk Flag, 1½x2 inches on 3½ inch Staff	.60
520/131	Silk Flag, 2x3 inches on 7 inch Staff	2.40
520/130	Silk Flag, 4x6 inches on 10½ inch Staff	4.50

DOZEN

32/142	Silk Flag, 4x6 inches on 13 inch Staff, Heavy Quality	$.80
23	Silk Flag, 6x8 inches on 24 inch White Wood Staff with Pulley and Stand.	4.50

WEDDING FAVORS AND NOVELTIES
WAX ORANGE BLOSSOM SPRAYS

93/527   75/102

		GROSS
75/202	Wax Orange Blossom Sprays, 1 Blossom, 1 Bud, 1 Leaf.........................	$4.50
75/201	Wax Orange Blossom Sprays, 1 Blossom, 3 Buds, 2 Leaves...................	8.40

		DOZEN
75/204	Wax Orange Blossom Sprays, 2 Blossoms, 4 Buds, 2 Leaves................	$1.20
75/203	Wax Orange Blossom Sprays, 1 Blossom, 6 Buds, 2 Leaves.................	1.20
75/200	Wax Orange Blossom Sprays, 3 Blossoms, 6 Buds, 3 Leaves...............	1.80
93/525	Wax Orange Blossom Sprays with Heavy Silver Leaf, 3 inches...........	1.20
93/526	Wax Orange Blossom Sprays with Heavy Gold Leaf, 3 inches.............	1.20
93/527	Wax Orange Blossom Sprays with White Satin Ribbon Bow, 3 inches	2.00
93/533	Wax Orange Blossom Bouquet with White Satin Ribbon Rosette, 3½ inches	4.00
93/524	Silver Metal Bell with Orange Blossom Spray and Satin Ribbon Bow, 1½ inches.	1.00
93/522	Gold Metal Wishbone with Orange Blossom Spray and Satin Ribbon Rosette, 4 inches.	1.50
93/520	Silver Horseshoe with Orange Blossom Spray and Satin Ribbon Rosette, 1¾ inches.	1.20
93/523	Gold Metal Horseshoe with Orange Blossom Spray and Satin Ribbon Rosette, 4 inches.	1.60
93/521	White Paper Bell with Orange Blossom Spray and Satin Ribbon Rosette, 4 inches.	1.60
12011	Lily of the Valley Spray, White Linen Flowers and Green Leaves, 3 inches.	.40

WAX BRIDES AND GROOMS, ETC.

		PER 100
75/100	Wax Bride and Groom, 1¾ inches...	$12.00
75/101	Wax Bride and Groom, 2 inches..	15.00
75/102	Wax Bride and Groom, 2½ inches..	20.30
75/105	Wax Bride and Groom, Groom with High Hat, 1¾ inches....................	10.50
75/106	Wax Bride and Groom, Groom with High Hat, 2 inches........................	16.00
75/103	Wax Bride with Veil, 2 inches...	8.50
75/104	Wax Groom, 2 inches...	8.50
75/109	Wax Cupid with Bow and Arrow, 1½ inches..	9.00
75/107	Wax Cupid with Violin, 1½ inches..	9.00
75/108	Wax Cupid with Banjo, 1½ inches...	9.00
11815	White Wax Dove, 1 inch..	5.50
11816	White Wax Dove with Message, 1¾ inches...	8.00
11814	Wax Stork, 2½ inches...	9.00
11822	White Wax Lamb, Sitting Position, 1 inch...	6.25
11821	White Wax Dog, 1¼ inches..	7.50
11817	Wax Gnome Figures, Four Styles, Assorted Colors, 1¾ inches...........	7.50

WEDDING FAVORS AND NOVELTIES (Continued)

355/81   355/78   93/536

PER 100

355/20	Heart Shape Glazed Boxes with Satin Ribbon Bow and Orange Blossom, Pink or White, 2½ inches....................................	$9.00
355/80	Oblong White Glazed Wedding Cake Box with Orange Blossom Spray and Satin Ribbon Bow, 3x2 inches............................	10.00
355/78	White Wedding Bell Box, Decorated with Orange Blossom Spray and Satin Ribbon Bow, 3½ inches............................	9.00
355/81	White Wedding Traveling Bag with Orange Blossom Spray, 3 inches.	12.50
355/79	White Wedding Trunk with Orange Blossom Spray and Satin Ribbon Bow, 3 inches.	18.50

WEDDING CAKE BOXES

18SM	White Glazed Wedding Cake Box, Moire Finish, 3x2x1¼ inches.........	$4.50
O0F	White Glazed Wedding Cake Box, Fleur-de-Lis Design, 2½x2½x1 inches.	5.00
O/M	White Glazed Wedding Cake Box, Moire Finish, 3½x½x1 inches........	5.00
30SF	White Glazed Wedding Cake Box, Fleur-de-Lis Design, Telescope Cover, 3x2x1¼ inches.	6.25
30E	White Glazed Wedding Cake Box, Laurel Wreath Design, Telescope Cover, 3½x2½x1 inches.	8.00
30CC	White Glazed Wedding Cake Box, Floral Design, Telescope Cover, 4x1¾x1¼ inches.	7.00

All the above Wedding Cake Boxes are complete with Paper Liner and Paper Lace Top.

DOZEN

355/21	Satin Heart Box Padded Top, Pink and White, 3¼ inches..................	$2.60
93/549	Miniature Traveling Trunk Filled with Confetti and Decorated with Ribbon Bow, 2¼ inches.	2.40
93/550	Miniature Traveling Trunk with White China Cupid Mounted on Top and Tied with Ribbon Rosette, 2¼ inches....................	3.50
93/536	Wedding Cake Box, Decorated with Chiffon Bow and Assorted China Wedding Favors, 3x2x1½ inches...............................	4.20
93/540	Same as 93/536 but size 3¾x2¾x1¼ inches...............................	5.40

WEDDING SLIPPERS

DOZEN

16764	Crepe Paper Slippers, 2½ inches..	$.38
16750	Pressed Paper Slipper with Crepe Paper Bag for Filling, Pink or White, 3½ inches.	.65
16752	Pressed Paper Silver Slipper with Silk Bag, 3 inches....................	.90
16753	Pressed Paper Silver Slipper with Silk Bag, 4 inches....................	1.35
355/73	Crepe Paper Slipper, Pink and White, with Satin Bow and Gold Heel, 5½ inches.	2.16
355/74	Satin Slipper, White and Pink, with Satin Bow and Gold Heel, 5½ inches.	3.00
31/300W	White Celluloid Parasol, 2½ inches......................................	.70
31/301W	White Celluloid Parasol, 3½ inches......................................	.85
8838	White Celluloid Folding Fan, 3 inches....................................	.75
X4174	White Celluloid Folding Fan, 5½ inches..................................	1.90
12747/117	White China Doll Dressed as Bride and Groom, 1¾ inches...............	.85
10700	White China Doll Dressed as Bride with Crochet Dress, 1½ inches......	2.10
10701	White China Doll Dressed as Groom with Crochet Suit, 1½ inches......	2.10